M_N
IN THE
MAKING

KYLE BUTT, STAN BUTT JR. & J.D. SCHWARTZ

Produced and published by:

World Video Bible School®
25 Lantana Lane
Maxwell, Texas 78656

www.WVBS.org

Copyright © **2012**

ISBN- 978-0-9827455-7-1

Third printing.

Cover Design by: Jordan Moore
Layout Design: Clayton Mitchell and Branyon May

VOLUME PRICING:

Although the books are sold individually, they can be obtained in volume from World Video Bible School.

Serving the Church since 1986

wvbs.org

Table of Contents

Introduction

A few years ago three things happened in one day.

First, I helped my wife put together a Bible class lesson for teenage girls on the topic "How far is too far?" I came up with a pretty good-sized packet of material both from Scripture and from a number of class books that I had in my office that were written for teenage young people. All the books were written by women for young women. In a fairly extensive office library I did not, at that time, own one book written to teenage boys aspiring to Christian manhood. There might have been one out there, but I didn't own it. And to tell the truth, I hadn't even heard of it. On the other hand, there are a multitude of books written for young women. And on the question, "How far is too far?" I was very disappointed to read that most of these girls' books seemed to advise teenage girls that young men are like pawing animals that need to be chased off with a stick. Of course, I guess that shouldn't be surprising if that is the way most young men act. It bothered me, though, that I didn't have a book written by a Christian man for young men teaching them how act with discipline, responsibility, and leadership.

Second, on the very same day, my mother told me that her publisher was looking for someone to write a book for young men. They said they already had the title, the outline, and everything else. They were just desperate for someone to write it. I was amused and remarked on the strange coincidence that I had just, that day, been thinking about the need for just such a book.

Third, (and here's the clincher), on the same day, in the middle of the same conversation, I received a phone call from a family friend in tears who told me that her daughter had just been raped by a boy in her class. I was devastated. I was so sad for the girl, her family, and I was sad for the boy—all the boys, really, out there awkwardly and often without much help on their way to becoming men. Who had failed these boys? Where had we gone wrong? Who was teaching our boys that it's ok to act like animals? Where had our boys missed learning about respect, discipline, purity, honor, self-control, and compassion? As a preacher and youth minister, I felt that I was to blame. As a father, I felt that I was to blame. And as a Christian man, I felt that I was to blame.

And so, several years after that strange day, after having mulled over what needed to be said, after having prayed about the needs, after being asked literally dozens of times if I knew where somebody could get a good book for Christian young men, and after recruiting some very able help, here it is.

Out of my sense of guilt for personal failure and a deep-seated belief that our young men need to be taught about Manhood instead of just stumbling into it, comes this book—*Men in the Making*. And make no mistake, I'm not just talking about making adult males. There are now more than 7 billion people on the planet. Just under half of those are males. There are lots of men in this world. But I'm talking about Real Men. I'm talking about God's Men. There's a difference. A big difference. Look at Paul's words at the top of this introduction. Paul is saying that any old male can be a "mere man," but Men of God, Real Men, well that's something special. These days it's extraordinary.

If you're not interested, put this book down right now. You're not ready for it.

But…

If being that kind of man sounds good to you, please read on, and May God bless you for it.

SB

DEDICATION

This book is dedicated to all of our sons and nephews with the hopes and prayers that they will grow to be great men of God: Drew Butt, Reed Butt, Nathan Butt, Nolan Butt, Wyatt Briceño, Lane Schwartz, John Thomas, Daniel Thomas, Nathan Thomas, Matthew Thomas, Ben Baker, and Ezekiel Baker.

CHAPTER 1

"To Be Or Not To Be?" That Is NOT The Question

"Just as the child is father to the man, so the impressions of one's youth remain the most vivid in manhood." (Gustav Stresseman)

"But we all with unveiled face, beholding as in a mirror the glory of the Lord are being transformed...." (2 Corinthians 3:18)

If you're reading this, hopefully you're a teenage boy who wants, one day, to be able to stand up, bang yourself on the chest, and proclaim confidently, "Now I am a Man." Or maybe you haven't thought that much about it. Maybe you're just scraping by: going from school to practice, to work, to home, to church, etc., etc., blah blah blah. Maybe you haven't given one thought to the type of man you want to be. Or maybe you are struggling with the inevitability of manhood that is being forced on you because you're graduating and moving out of the house or because you have suddenly, unexpectedly become the "man of the house." You know Manhood is coming. In fact it's just around the corner, but you're not sure that you are ready for it. If any of this describes you, then this book is for you, because it's about becoming a Man—whether you want to or not. Whether you're ready for it or not. Because, in reality, that is what happens. Nobody asks your permission. Nobody asks if you are ready. Nobody even asks if you want it.

In other cultures there are clear lines that mark the transition between Boyhood and Manhood. Usually some physical or spiritual ritual clearly marks the event. A male might say, for instance, "In the summer of my seventeenth year, I became a man."

What do you think are the benefits of such a cultural tradition? What might be some disadvantages?

1

More primitive cultures usually mark this transition with some kind of physical test—a very difficult journey, capturing an eagle feather, killing a bear or boar, spending a week in the wilderness. You get the idea. Because of the young male's successful completion of a certain test, he has a definite moment that he can identify as his Manhood moment. As dangerous as these tests might be, they serve a vital purpose in letting the boy know that he is now expected to think and act like a man—a very important landmark (1 Corinthians 13:11).

Generally speaking, American boys do not have to survive some dangerous Manhood ritual. It might be better if we did. We are plagued with the questions, "Am I a man now?" "When will I be a man?" "How will I know when I'm a man?" Because of this nagging doubt some American sub-cultures have established their own rites of passage into Manhood. Some of these include: losing your virginity, fathering a child, gang-raping a woman, killing a person, or taking drugs for the first time. Tragically, an 11-year-old could do any of these. Do you honestly think that any of these things can turn you into a man? Being a Man is different from being "the man." If these are the tests of Manhood in America we shouldn't wonder that the state of Manhood has sunk to an all-time low.

If you had to say one thing that our culture views as a "rite to manhood," what would you say it is?

From Boyhood to Manhood

That leaves us with the basic problems: 1) We don't know how to get from Boyhood to Manhood; and, 2) We're not sure we'd recognize Manhood if we got there. Edward Abbey said, "In the modern techno-industrial culture, it is possible to proceed from infancy to senility without ever knowing manhood." What a tragedy!

Because of our inability to mark our transition from Boyhood to Manhood, we struggle with irresponsibility, immaturity, and self-doubt. I am well into my thirties (in fact, pushing 40), working on my second decade of marriage, and I have two teenage daughters. Almost anybody would say that I had made the transition from Boyhood to Manhood. But even though that's true, I have no idea exactly how or when that happened. I think I missed something.

That's because the transition from Boyhood to Manhood is a process. It starts on the day we males are born. Arriving in this world with a particular set of genes, many details of our identity are pretty well fixed from birth: height, hair color, eye color, skin color, and so on. Nutrition and environment combine with the genetic factors to shape the growing process. Every individual with whom we come in contact makes some contribution to our becoming men. Parents, grandparents, siblings, teachers, coaches, friends, girlfriends, the lunch lady, the preacher—all leave impressions on us that shape us in some way from the day we are born.

Then puberty comes around. Our bodies change. But even puberty doesn't have a clear starting and stopping point. A few zits (or a lot) arrive along with hair in some strange places, but zits and quantities of mysterious hair keep showing up throughout a man's life. Our priorities and ideals change while we're in puberty. Girls go from having things we don't like, "cooties" for instance, to having things we do like. We notice these changes, and we're not at all sure how we feel about it. Then, suddenly, we are very sure how we feel about it. The transitions and changes in our lives don't end there, though. People start pressuring us to do things. We want to be a part of the "in crowd." We want to have fun and be accepted. But something in the back of our minds tells us there's more to life than having fun. Driver's license tests, beer runs, drag racing, a joint, a fight in the locker room, betting on sports, dance parties, backseats of cars, "listening to music" in your girlfriend's bedroom. Every day you will make important decisions about how to handle these situations and hundreds more like them. Which desires will you satisfy?—the desires to do what is responsible and right?—or the desires to give in to your weakness for the sake of fun and pleasure?

Your Actions Matter—Now

This is where "the rubber meets the road," so to speak. This is the battleground on which the war is waged for our Manhood. Let me explain. Someone is trying to sell you the idea that your life as a teenager doesn't have anything to do with your life as an adult. "Sow your wild oats." "Have fun now. There'll be time enough for grown-up stuff later." "You don't have to act

3

like a man. You're just a kid." "Try this." "Try that." "Smoke this." "Drink this." "Everybody does this when he's growing up." "Boys will be boys." "It's ok. It's expected that teenage boys will act like this." "Teenage years are for experimenting." "It's only natural." In fact, there is currently a very popular song titled "Young, Wild, and Free." The lyrics of the chorus go like this: "So what we get drunk? So what we smoke weed? We're just having fun. We don't care who sees. So what we go out? That's how it's supposed to be, living young and wild and free." Does that stuff sound familiar? (Take a second to compare these lines to one from the Bible: 1 Timothy 4:12.)

Read Ecclesiastes 11:9. How does this verse relate to the idea of "sowing your wild oats?"

Tragically, many teenage boys buy into these deceptions. They believe that the consequences of their teenage decisions will somehow magically vanish when they enter adulthood—as if their chalkboard is magically erased when they graduate from high school. Here's a newsflash! The habits and thoughts you have now, you will carry with you into Manhood. The language you use now, you'll use as an adult. If you become an alcoholic or drug addict in high school, you will fight it until you die. If you treat sex casually and recreationally, your life will be full of empty, hollow relationships. A police record from your teenage years will haunt you for your entire life—just like sexually transmitted diseases, car wrecks, and the consequences of thousands of other decisions that didn't seem to be such a big deal at the time. Welcome to the real world.

Think about a time in your life when you realized that your actions have real consequences.

Because THIS is IT. Every day of our lives we are becoming the Men we will be tomorrow. I am. You are. Whether you are 13 or 30, the Man you are today will be the most influential individual in making the Man you will be tomorrow. You can't take a time out. You can't hide behind your youth. You can't say, "I'm not ready." Like it or not, you are already in the process of becoming the Man you will be. And

4

every second counts—as does every word, every thought, every action, every choice.

There is only one person responsible for the Man you are becoming. Guess who. Need a hint? Look in the mirror. Yeah, it's YOU. Not a parent, not a teacher, not a coach, not a warden, not a drill sergeant, not a woman. YOU will construct your own Manhood. With God's help and instruction, you can be the Man you want and need to be.

> What are some ways that the internet, social networking, camera phones, and other technology can magnify the consequences of your actions—for good or evil?

That sounds like a pretty big job doesn't it? What? You're not sure if you're ready for it yet? Sorry. I wish I could say that you don't need to worry about this stuff until you're 20, or maybe 18, at the earliest, but that is not the truth.

Do you remember how birthdays felt when you were a little kid? Did 10 really feel any different than being 9? No? Did you ever feel

> Discuss what characteristics you believe define a real Man.

any older or different on the day of your birthday than you did the day before? No? Nobody ever does! That's what I'm trying to tell you. You are not going to go to sleep one night as a Boy and wake up the next morning as a Man.

You are Not going to Become a Man One Day.

You ARE BECOMING a Man EVERY Day.

SB

5

Tools for Real Men
Helping to measure up

THE TRUTH ABOUT MORAL ISSUES

Topics: Lying, Dancing, Drinking, Gambling, Pornography, Modesty, and Tattoos & Piercings

Sooner or later, most of us find ourselves facing moral, social, and ethical situations. These situations affect our family and friends. This video series provides compelling and informative answers from a biblical and practical standpoint.

video.wvbs.org

GOD'S PLAN FOR SAVING MAN

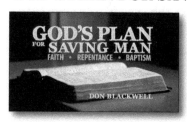

God has a plan for saving man from sin. This plan involves His Son, Jesus, and the gift He has offered. The Bible discusses man's obedience to God's will, explaining the concepts of faith, grace, repentance, and baptism. Follow along with Don Blackwell as he looks at what the Bible has to say about God's plan.

video.wvbs.org

SOCIAL MEDIA EVANGELISM

This five-minute program features Reagan Garner explaining some ideas and ways people can use social media to teach and evangelize their friends, family and others using WVBS material. It is an excellent short lesson to show to young and old alike.

video.wvbs.org

CHAPTER 2

Why Don't You Just Grow Up?

"In the meanest are all the materials of manhood, only they are not rightly disposed." (Henry David Thoreau)

"When I was a child, I spoke as a child, I understood as a child, I thought as a child; but when I became a man I put away childish things." (1 Corinthians 13:11)

"Why don't you just grow up?"

Who's asked you that question in the last year? Your parents? A girl? Your big sister? It's one of those questions we detest. We hate it. And we hear it over and over and over again during our teenage years. American teenagers have a reputation for being selfish, rude, and irresponsible. And although I've known many who fit that description perfectly, I've known just as many who were compassionate, courteous, and dependable. The problem is that we often live up to the expectations that everyone seems to have for us. If society expects teens to be reckless, apathetic, and smart-mouthed, then who are we to disappoint? Because of these reputations and expectations we somehow start to believe that it is ok to act just like that.

> List some qualities and characteristics of a mature person. Of an immature person.

But it's not ok; not ok at all. God's word sets forth a distinctly different set of expectations for young men.

"Let no one look down on your youth, but be an example to the believers in word, in conduct, in love, in spirit, in faith, in purity." (Paul, 1 Timothy 4:12)

"Rejoice, O young man, in your youth, and let your heart cheer you in the days of your youth, walk in the impulses of your heart, and as you see to be best; but know that for all these God will bring you into judgment. Therefore remove vexation from your heart and put away evil from your flesh, for childhood and youth are vanity. Remember now your Creator in the days of your youth...." (Solomon, Ecclesiastes 11:9-12:1)

"... I have written to you, young men, because you are strong, and the word of God abides in you, and you have overcome the wicked one." (John, 2 John 1:14)

"My son, pay attention to my wisdom; lend your ear to my understanding, that you may preserve discretion, and your lips may keep knowledge." (Solomon, Proverbs 5:1-2)

Where's the rudeness? The recklessness? The selfishness and apathy? Not there, are they? You see, although the world may expect you as a teenage male to act like that, God doesn't. That behavior and those attitudes are absolutely unacceptable for you as a young Christian.

> **What are some of the "benefits" of acting immaturely? Why do you think so many young people act this way?**

Any builder worth his salt will tell you that a building is only as good as its foundation. If the foundation is weak, the building is weak. Solomon, Paul, John, and others realized that maturity in young men lays a vital foundation for their spirituality the rest of their lives. In the course of this study, we will discuss some of the greatest heroes of the Bible, but most of these men were strong because they made a commitment to faithfulness as young men. You've heard of Daniel, David, Joseph, Joshua, and Jesus I assume. All faithful Men—who before that were faithful Young Men. Daniel had the courage to break an unjust law about prayer, because he always prayed three times every day "as was his custom since youth." On the day David killed the Philistine giant Goliath he was ridiculed by his

> **When you look at the stories of young men who were heroes in the Bible, what characteristics did they have that helped them?**

8

brother Eliab, King Saul, and Goliath for his youth and inexperience, and yet through this young man the Lord won a great victory for Israel. Joseph at age seventeen was able to resist the seduction of a rich and powerful woman to become, through God's providence, the savior of two nations. Moses, in his youth, made the decision to turn his back on the power and pleasures of Pharaoh's palace to cast his lot with God's people. Joshua, as a young spy, bucked the tide of peer pressure to declare that God would indeed give the Israelites victory in the promised land; and he would later become the great general who would lead them to that victory. Jesus was debating religion in the Temple as a twelve year-old. He grew in wisdom, and size, and in favor with God and man; and He is now seated at the right hand of God. What do all these great men have in common? They were all, at one point in their lives, faithful teenagers who recognized their spiritual responsibilities as Men of God even when some still considered them boys.

> Many of the heroes of the Bible committed sins as well. What characteristics caused them to stumble?

"Rome wasn't built in a day."

"The mightiest oak tree doesn't sprout from the ground fully grown in a year or two, or ten, or twenty." And Men of God don't rise fully mature on their eighteenth or twenty-first birthday. Please realize that you have the responsibility of being a Man of God NOW. You are responsible for your

> How can the stories of Bible characters help you find the strength to do right? Read Hebrews 12:1.

conduct, your influence, and your salvation. You may not be old enough to vote, be drafted, buy cigarettes or drink beer. But none of these things ever made a man. Some may still think of you as a boy and treat you disrespectfully because of it. Older people have enough biases about teenagers as it is. How about being one of those extraordinary individuals who restores people's faith in the promise and prospect of all young people and reassures them of the bright future of the Lord's Church?

SB

9

Tools for Real Men
Helping to measure up

THE TRUTH ABOUT BIBLE STUDY

"Bible Study" covers the importance of studying God's Word. How can Christians provide reasoned answers and guidance to friends without proper study and contemplation?

video.wvbs.org

THE STORY OF MOSES

Glenn Colley effectively weaves the events of Moses' life: from the providential care as a young baby, through the dramatic Egyptian exodus, to Moses' mountain-top death at the edge of the Promised Land. After watching these three segments, you will come away with a deep appreciation of God's relationship with His faithful people.

video.wvbs.org

TRANSFORMED: A SPIRITUAL JOURNEY

What does it mean to be searching for truth? Find out as you go on an exciting, personal journey with Lance Mosher. *Transformed* tells one man's true spiritual journey, as he encounters the various moments of life that made him question everything he had been taught; the very essence of who he thought he was. His experiences will resonate with anyone who is looking for meaning in a world of chaos. This book is a great way to form a Bible study relationship with anyone. This 238-page, paperback book will entertain, encourage and evangelize.

www.wvbs.org

CHAPTER 3

What Do You Want To Be When You Grow Up?

"There goes the only man I ever admired. He's what every boy wants to be when he grows up, and what every old man wishes he had been." (The Tall Men)

"To this you were called, because Christ suffered for you, leaving you an example, that you should follow His steps." (1 Peter 2:21)

When I was thirteen years old, I wallpapered my own bedroom. It took me months and probably cost me a couple hundred bucks of my own hard-earned money. But it was finally done. And it was beautiful…at least to me. Nobody else seemed to like it much… especially grandparents who might visit and sleep in my room. You see, covering every square inch of wall in my bedroom were pictures of professional basketball players. Most of the great players, and anyone else who could engineer an amazing dunk, all earned a prominent display on my walls. I had a picture of Dominic Wilkins' spectacular between-the-legs-behind-the-back-head-even-with-the-rim dunk. I had Spud Webb's Dunk-contest-winning dunk. But mostly I had pictures of Michael Jordan. Of all the posters in my room, more than half of them were of His Airness Himself. Michael Jordan was a legend—and still is. And I loved him. I even had a life-sized poster of him dunking—legs spread, tongue hanging out, everything. Man, that guy could play ball. And I wanted to be just like him.

I bought the shoes—the very first year they ever made Air Jordans. I watched the games. I read the articles. I learned everything a thirteen-year-old boy could learn about Michael Jordan. For instance, I knew that Michael Jordan once got cut from his high school basketball team (which was very encouraging to me, since I wasn't that good). I knew that Michael Jordan dunked his first basketball as a sophomore. I knew that Michael Jordan was so quick off the dribble that his college coach had to make a special video for the referees just to demonstrate to them that he wasn't traveling.

When I was thirteen years old, I wanted to be just like Mike.

Name a Man who you would like to be like when you grow up. Why did you pick him?

Who do you want to be like? Lebron James? Ben Rothlisberger? Tiger Woods? Derek Jeter? You've got somebody picked out. Who is it? Maybe it's not somebody famous. Maybe it's somebody at school—some guy a few years older than you, captain of the football team, looks cool, acts cool, dresses cool, great looking girlfriend, nice truck—you know the guy.

Here's the thing about role models though: the older you get, the more you realize that those guys just don't have it altogether like you thought they did. M.J. gets old and retires—for the last time. Kobe and Big Ben are accused of rape. Tiger Woods is still sorting out his mess. The guy at school—he's a drunk who's barely going to graduate and will probably be lucky to get a job holding a "SLOW" sign on a county road construction crew.

Real Role Models

If we're going to have role models, we need to do a little better than that.

Why do you believe examples and role models are so important?

We need people to pattern our lives after. Don't get me wrong. I like them. But football, basketball, baseball, and skateboarding are not life, despite what the t-shirt might say.

Life is about priorities, character, being a husband, a father, a friend, a son. It's about defining success and pursuing it. It's about faith, hope, and love. Solomon concluded that life is "fearing God and keeping His commandments for this is the whole of man." Those are the last and only things that matter. And guess what: you're not going to learn much about those things from the typical role models that are available today.

Let me suggest three categories of worthy role models for Christian young men.

Just Plain Christian Men

First, there are those Men in our lives who set worthy examples of Christian Manhood. For me, there were coaches: Mike Maples, basketball coach, Bible teacher, and missionary; Marty Avery, football coach, godly father, Bible teacher, and preacher; Rick Barker, football and tennis coach, godly husband, father, grandfather, and elder of the the Lord's Church. There were teachers like Carl Pierson and David Davidson. There were preachers like Marlin Connelly, Mike Greene, John Vaughn, Billy Smith, and Tom Holland. There were youth ministers like David Craig, Jeff Ingram, Kevin White, and Jerry Elder. There were elders: Johnny Knott, Robert Waddell, and Ed Daughrity.

Then there were just plain Men. You know them. Christian Men who love their wives and children, who are strong and stable, who laugh and love and work and play and worship. They've lived longer than you have. They know more than you do. They've been through trials and come out again. They're wise and godly and you want to be just like them. I think of Cal Praither and Jack Logue. I think of Glen Kinnard and Charles and Billy Curtis. I think about my father-in-law David Harmon, a Vietnam veteran, a brilliant engineer, a godly man

> **Read Philippians 3:17-18. What was Paul urging his readers to do? What was he urging his readers to avoid doing?**

and elder of the Lord's Church who has struggled every day for the last decade with cancer and chemo but never utters one complaint and is always cheerful and faithful and is one of the lighthouses of my life. I think about my Dad. I pray to God that you had the kind of father that you could look up to and admire. Dad never has accomplished anything earth-shattering. Chances are you won't read about my Dad in any history book. Oh, he's had his share of successes and his share of failures, but through it all my father's example of strength and honesty and uncompromising Christianity has been another of the lighthouses of my life. I don't write this list of Men to drag you through a personal tribute but to show you that there are in fact, Heroes all around you. There are men worthy of your respect and emulation.

As you grow older though, you'll learn more about these Men who are your heroes. Sometimes you'll learn more than you want to learn. Some of the things you'll learn will probably disappoint you. These Men, although it may not seem so now, are just human; and humans have faults. They stumble. They sin. They fall. Just like you do. But these Everyday Heroes, for all their faults, are bound to be better role models than ball players, rappers, actors, and Mr. Football with the good-looking girlfriend. Because when it's all said and done, I hope you'll pick role models whose examples will help you get into heaven and not lead you into hell.

Men of Renown in the Bible

Another place to find worthy role models is in the pages of the Bible. Noah was a great father and servant of God. Abraham demonstrated faith and courage. Jacob was wise, tough, and trusted the Lord to care for him. Joseph was committed to doing right no matter the cost. Moses was perhaps the greatest leader of men who ever lived. Joshua was a brilliant spy, soldier, and general. Gideon, Samson, Daniel, Peter, Paul, Timothy, Titus, John...the list goes on and on. Paul wrote to Timothy and encouraged him to "study to show yourself approved unto God, a workman that needs not be ashamed." By studying God's Word we learn these great stories of faith, courage, obedience, and victory. We can strengthen ourselves with the godly role models in the pages of Scripture.

> Read 1 Peter 2:21. What does this verse say was one of the primary reasons that Jesus came to the Earth?

The Man—Jesus Christ

Lastly, there is the model of Christ for us to follow. Christ's attitudes and actions are the very essence of what we are seeking to become. Paul himself urged his students to "Imitate me, just as

14

I imitate Christ." The highest honor we can ever hope to hold is to wear the name of Christ, to have our lives remind others of Him, to bring glory, honor, and lost souls to Him through our examples. There is no greater task. There is no more worthwhile venture. There is no greater hero than Jesus Christ. Sometimes artists give us the impression that Jesus was some pale, weak, beautiful person who'd never done a hard day's work in His life. But this is not the Jesus of the Bible. He was hardworking and rugged. He was tough and violent at times. He was sinless, wise, brave, strong, compassionate, prayerful, humble, powerful, and loving. If we are not attempting to follow in His footprints, we're headed to the wrong place.

Worldly role models are rich, popular, and sometimes powerful, but they're also shallow, superficial, and silly compared to good Christian Men, Bible heroes, and Jesus Christ. We don't need posters of our heroes. We don't need autographs or special shoes. We just need to open our eyes, refocus our priorities and recognize the heroes that we see all around us.

SB

Tools for Real Men
Helping to measure up

BEHOLD! THE LAMB OF GOD

This is the second seminar in the *Pillars of Faith* series and explores the historicity, deity and personality of Christ. It is hosted by Kyle Butt and Eric Lyons, and includes 6 lessons.

video.wvbs.org

FOLLOWING CHRIST CLOSELY: A STUDY OF DISCIPLESHIP

As we journey through our Christian life, we should always seek to imitate Christ. It should be our ultimate goal in life to be His disciples and in so being, we should be Christ-like. Join Mike Vestal in the lesson as he presents a lesson on the Bible topic of discipleship.

video.wvbs.org

THE BIBLICAL ACCOUNT OF NOAH

Noah was born into a sinful and morally unraveling world. The Bible describes a world filled with violence, wickedness and corruption. How did the world fall into such awful conditions? What were the challenges that faced Noah and his wife, as they tried to raise their family?

What was the path God wanted them to follow? Consider the biblical account of Noah's life and response to God.

video.wvbs.org

WHO IS JESUS? | SEARCH JESUS

Who is Jesus? To say that He's the most famous person in the world is an understatement. He lived almost two thousand years ago, and yet His name is still one of the most often searched for words on the Internet. Some skeptics question His existence entirely, and atheists don't believe in him at all. What's the truth about Jesus?

video.wvbs.org

Tuition-Free, Online Bible Education

ONLINE BIBLE SCHOOL

And the things that you have heard from me among many witnesses, commit these to faithful men who will be able to teach others also. 2 Timothy 2:2

16

CHAPTER 4

The Church of Today

"Old age is like everything else. To make a success of it, you've got to start young." (Theodore Roosevelt)

"Do not say, 'I am a youth,' for you shall go to all to whom I send you." (Jeremiah 1:7)

Most of us have been in a worship service when this has happened: an older gentleman scheduled to lead the opening prayer for a Sunday night service walks to the podium and begins praying. In the course of the prayer, he asks the Lord to be with the teenagers of the congregation since "they are the church of tomorrow." This phrase is one of those "favorite" clichés that often gets repeated in prayers. This "church of tomorrow" concept suggests that teenagers are "second string" players who are sitting on the sidelines, waiting their turn to get in the game. It's as if teens' actions, words, and contributions to the church don't really count now, but one day they will. The problem with this idea, however, is that it couldn't be more wrong.

If you have been baptized into Christ, you are just as important a member of the Lord's Church as anybody younger or older than you. There are no players on the bench in the Lord's Church. Your actions, words, and contributions can be just as helpful, or harmful, to the Lord's cause as any other member, regardless of age. Teenage Christians are not the Church of tomorrow, they are the Church of today.

> **Why is the phrase "the church of tomorrow" not an accurate description for teens?**

Think About Who Does What

The other day I was speaking at a youth rally and a young man approached me after the lesson. He mentioned that he was having serious doubts about God and the Bible, but his friend in the youth group had invited him to this particular event. He said that the lessons that had been presented changed his life and really helped him realize that God is real. If it hadn't been for his friend in this youth group, this young man might have continued in his path of doubt and atheism for the rest of his life. When we look at what group of people in the Church is inviting their friends to hear the truth, and standing up for God's Word on a daily basis, we see that teens often are more active than any other group in the Church. Teenagers are some of the most enthusiastic, productive evangelists in many congregations around the world.

In fact, what group travels hundreds of miles to knock doors and help smaller congregations put on Vacation Bible Schools and evangelistic campaigns? Teenagers. Who often makes up a large part of the Summer mission teams that go to foreign countries and conduct medical mission trips? Teens. Who pours countless hours into after school devos, lock ins, youth retreats, Bible studies, and Internet blogs and texts about God, Jesus, and the Church? Teens. While we are not in any way trying to disparage what the older people of the Lord's Church are doing, it is a fact that many times, the most productive workers in the Church are teenagers.

> In your congregation, what are some things that young Christians can be involved in?

That's How It's Always Been

The fact that teens are often some of the most vital, productive workers in the Lord's Kingdom is nothing new. As you look into the Bible, you see that teenagers have always been a crucial component in God's plans. Many of the most memorable stories in the Old Testament involve teens who were dedicated to God's cause. For instance, when David was "but a youth," he visited his brothers in the camp of Saul. During his visit, he saw a giant

Philistine almost 10-feet tall who taunted the Lord's people. He was astonished that none of the older soldiers in the Lord's army were willing to fight the giant who was mocking God and His people. Even King Saul was scared to fight the menacing Philistine. When David told Saul that he would fight the giant, Saul told David that he was not able to fight the giant because he was just a youth (1 Samuel 17:33). The word "youth" in this verse mostly likely means a teenager or a person not much older than 20 years old. You, of course, know that David did not think his youthfulness was a hindrance and neither did God. God used the young man David to kill Goliath, rout the Philistines, and bring honor to His name. David was not "the army of tomorrow." He happened to be the only soldier that was willing to fight the battle that was happening right then.

The names Daniel, Shadrach, Meshach, and Abed-nego are quite familiar to all of us. These young men were most likely teenagers when they were ripped away from their homes in Judah and transplanted into the pagan, idolatrous land of Babylon. They were given every opportunity to forsake the Law of God that their parents had taught them and adopt the pagan, sinful ways of the Babylonians. But these young men purposed in their hearts that they would not forsake the God of their fathers, and their powerful stand for the Truth is recorded in the Bible as an example for all people, young and old, to follow.

Joseph was sold into Egypt when he was seventeen. In Egypt, he was elevated to be the head over Potiphar's house—an extremely prestigious position. Furthermore, Potiphar's wife tempted him on a daily basis to sin, yet Joseph would not yield to her. Eventually, God used Joseph to save all of Egypt, Canaan, and the Israelites through whom the Messiah would come. Some of Joseph's most valiant victories for God occurred when he was a teenager.

In the New Testament, we see God working through teenagers as well. Of all the women in human history that God could have chosen to be the earthly mother of Jesus, He chose Mary. Most historians believe that Mary was about 15 or 16 years old when the angel Gabriel announced to her that she was going to be the biological mother of the Messiah. Her faith in God's Word is a powerful testimony to the fact that God often uses teenagers to do some of the most important jobs in His Kingdom.

The apostle Paul repeatedly used the young preacher Timothy to do some of the most crucial tasks in the early Church. Paul knew that some members of the Church would think that Timothy's young age was a hindrance to his ability to be productive. Yet Paul knew that was not the truth. In fact, Paul told Timothy: "Let no one despise your youth, but be an example to the believers in word, in conduct, in love, in spirit, in faith, in purity" (1 Timothy 4:12). Not only was the young preacher an example to other people his age, but he was an example to the entire Church, both old and young alike. Furthermore, most historians believe that Titus was also a teenager (or not much older). Teens have been vital to the Lord's cause throughout human history.

> **List some other young people in the Bible who did great things (2 Chronicles 24:1-6 & Jeremiah 1:7)**

Alex's Lemonade Stand

In 1996, Alexandra Scott was born to Jay and Liz Scott in Manchester, Connecticut. Just before her first birthday, she was diagnosed with neuroblastoma, a very serious childhood cancer. She battled the cancer for four years, and was given a special treatment in 2000. While in the hospital, she told her mother that she wanted to set up a lemonade stand in her front yard to help raise money to give to the doctors who helped her, so that they could try to find a cure for cancer. True to her word, when she was released from the hospital, she set up a lemonade stand in her front yard and raised $2,000 that year, which she gave to the hospital. Each year she continued to set up her stand, and each year the proceeds from her sales grew. Others heard about her courageous

> **What qualities do teenage young men like yourselves possess that God can use to build up His Church?**

fight against cancer, and her desire to raise money to find a cure for the dreaded disease. Soon, hundreds of "Alex's Lemonade Stands" across the country were raising hundreds of thousands of dollars each year. Tragically, in 2004, Alex died of cancer at eight years old. But before she died, she knew that her efforts had helped inspire others to raise over one million dollars to fight cancer. Furthermore, Alex's Lemonade Stand Foundation, to date, has raised over 30 million dollars and funded over 100 research projects in efforts to fight cancer. A four-year-old with a vision changed the world forever. Your age is not nearly as important as your desire to see the Lord's Kingdom spread. What can you do as a teenager, not tomorrow, but today, that will change the world forever?

KB

Tools for Real Men
Helping to measure up

SEARCHING FOR TRUTH: ABOUT THE CHURCH

The word church is used well over one hundred times in the New Testament. It is obviously a very important word but what does it mean? And, does Jesus have a church to which we must belong in order to be saved?

searchingfortruth.org

21

PASSAGE 6 | JUDAH: DAVID'S TESTING GROUND OF FAITH

Filmed on location, the film examines the historical account and poetic literature associated with one of Israel's greatest heroes, and how the terrain, climate, and environs of Judah served as an important element in shaping his faith. This Passage will forever change the way you read the Bible, and especially the Psalms. By watching this unique presentation on the interrelationship between the land of Israel and the people who lived there, you will find yourself being strengthened in faith and better prepared to meet your own personal trials and hardships.

biblelandpassages.org

MEN'S TRAINING COURSE

This series of lessons was designed and presented by Kevin Rutherford to help men be better leaders in the worship assembly. These lessons cover the principles of worship, pattern of worship, preaching in worship, presiding at the Lord's table, prayer and song leading. This course includes 6 lessons on 2 DVDs.

www.wvbs.org

GOD'S KINGDOM

"God's Kingdom" is a 5-part story about three friends planning to take a summer hiking trip around Europe. Before the trip Steve, a new Christian, asks his friend Bill, who hikes in the area, to take him and a couple of friends hiking on the local trails to get themselves in shape for their summer trip. Bill is glad to be of help and over the next few weeks Bill has an opportunity to talk with Kevin and his sister Kathy about the kingdom of God found in the Bible.

video.wvbs.org

CHAPTER 5

Honoring
the Older

"For age is opportunity no less
Than youth itself, though in another dress,
And as the evening twilight fades away
The sky is filled with stars, invisible by day."
(Henry Wadsworth Longfellow)

"You shall rise before the gray headed and honor the presence of an
old man, and fear your God...." (Leviticus 19:32)

You've heard it before, all about how your parents and grandparents used to walk to a one-room schoolhouse, uphill both ways, barefooted, and in the snow. Even though we smirk at these humorous exaggerations–that it always snowed in Tennessee (that's where I grew up, and we were lucky to see one or two snowfalls a year), or that you could walk uphill going to and from–there seems to be a reminiscence of a different time that no longer exists.

> **What are some changes you've seen in just 5-10 years? What are some other changes you've heard your grandparents talk about?**

You know what? They are right! We do live in a different time in which things are far removed from what they once were… and that is ok! As our world continues to change, we must figure out how to adapt and thrive. There are certain things, however, that must never change when it comes to our faith in God and how that faith is manifested on a daily basis. No matter what things are changing around us, God intended for His word in our lives to be transcendent. In other words, God's word is

ALWAYS relevant (1 Peter 1:25). It teaches us how to live in every culture and in all surroundings.

One of the biggest things that has changed in our culture is an overall lack of respect for people. Although, in this chapter, we will focus specifically on our respect and honor for those who are older, I want to ask a couple of questions in order to help you understand the honor and respect I'm talking about. When was the last time you opened a door for a girl or a woman of any age? I hope you can say that you always do, but chances are, you might not have even thought about opening the door for a female. When was the last time you took your hat off indoors? That's an old courtesy that's pretty much a non-factor these days, and I'm ok with the fact that wearing hats indoors isn't seen as a disrespectful gesture. However, I would challenge us to think about our respect for the Lord in this instance. We ought to always take our hats off in reverence before the Lord in any act of worship towards Him.

What is the first thought that comes to your mind when you see or think about an "old person?"

Have you ever taken an apple–or some other gift of appreciation–to one of your school teachers? I dare say you haven't since elementary school at least. Have you ever stood to greet a woman or elderly person when they walk into a room? Have you ever helped an older person with their groceries or to their car? Chances are you don't think about these things regularly, and I can tell you that these things are not at the forefront of my mind either. We just don't think about these types of actions in conjunction with our honor and respect for people, especially older people. But we should! Whether someone is 15, 20, or 50 years older than we are, we ought to have a level of respect for that person that shows in our actions toward that person.

Interestingly, the Bible has a lot to say about the attitude of respect we should have for those who are older than us. Now, I'm not talking about an older sibling who tries to demand your respect just because he or she is "older than you are." I'm talking about those people who are genuinely older and more experienced in life, and therefore, they deserve to be treated with honor and respect.

Are All Older People Worthy of Honor?

Not everyone who is older is deserving of honor. There are many who have wasted their lives chasing after immature dreams and pleasures. They never grew up, or worse, they destroyed themselves and everyone around them. All they ever did was leave a trail of hurt behind them. You can see that trail of pain throughout their long lives.

Are they deserving of honor and respect? Maybe not…but remember that we are called to treat people as Jesus would. Jesus never turned away anyone in His compassion for souls, and neither should we.

How do you feel about being expected to show respect even if someone doesn't deserve it? Why do you think God wants us to show it no matter what?

We also know older authority figures in our schools and jobs who seem to mistreat and misuse their power. They hurt us and talk down at us. They seem to enjoy walking all over people who are weaker than they are. Do they deserve honor and respect? Probably not…but Jesus doesn't ask us to behave in reaction to others. He asks us to live in His image. Therefore, we give the honor and respect that they don't deserve. I would simply challenge you to give honor and respect to those who are older than you no matter what the circumstances are, simply because you are called to "walk worthy of the calling to which you have been called, with all lowliness…" (Ephesians 4:1). Always strive to lift up others above yourself.

The Good News

Fortunately, there will be, and probably already are, some amazing, older people in your life that are deserving of your honor and respect. These are men and women who love you and are genuinely concerned about your well-being. They have proven themselves in life and in relationships, and you/I/we should be honoring them.

I wonder why we often neglect to honor those who are so deserving. If you really stop and think about our culture's idea of honor and respect, you might even be ashamed of the fact that often our honors are based on trivial and meaningless events and achievements in a person's life. We respect the man who hits the most home runs in a single season. We respect the man with the most tackles in a single season. Blake Griffin is a "beast," because he jumped over a car to win the 2011 NBA dunk contest. Michael Phelps is the most decorated Olympic swimmer ever and world record holder in several swimming events. Halls of Fame are filled with athletes who achieved something big on the turf. Every day we tune in to ESPN to see what other athletic accomplishments have taken place. I love sports, and I respect those guys who are athletic phenoms. Watching these people do what they do is cool! Our culture respects movie stars, singers, and models. All of these accomplishments are "great," and so we give these people honor and respect! But what do these accomplishments mean in the long run?

Name someone else you admire because of their talents and abilities.

On the other hand, there are men and women who have given their lives and livelihoods to serve our country and give us freedom. We say we honor them, but that honor usually only takes place on one specific day in the year, Veterans Day. We have parents, grandparents, and others who have surrounded us in love. Have you honored these people in your life lately? What about all those people in the nursing homes? Now, I'll be the first to tell you that going to a nursing home is a difficult thing for me. The smells are hard to stomach, and the awkward stares you get from people are…well…awkward.

Who is the older man or woman in your life that you respect the most? Why?

I remember eating with a good friend in a nursing home. He had asked me several times to come eat lunch as his guest. I enjoyed the company and the visit, but the meal was difficult. Every time he tried to put food in his mouth, some of it would come right back out onto his clothes. Needless to say, it was hard to eat my own meal without having my food come back up. In spite of the indignities, many of these people are worthy of honor, because of the way in which they lived their lives in service and love toward others. We are blessed with the opportunity to give it.

The point is that we must give honor and respect to those who deserve it, because they have gained wisdom and struggled through experiences of both failure and success. And now, they want to share it with you.

The Honored and Respected

There are actually different types of older people in the Bible that God says are deserving of honor and respect. The first would be those that were given a special task by God. I want you to think about men like Noah, Abraham, Moses, Joshua, David, Elijah, Elisha, Daniel, Peter, Paul, and John (just to name a few). Consider women like Sarah, Rahab, Ruth, Mary, Elizabeth, and Anna (check out Luke 3). These were men and women who had a special place in God's plan, and in some cases, they were even asked to be God's mouthpieces with a special message for His people. There are men and women in your life right now that God has placed in your life for your guidance. He may not have a specific individual message that they are supposed to bring you, but they may have such knowledge of God's word and His wisdom in their lives, that you need to pay attention to them. I think about parents and Bible class teachers. I think about your preacher or youth minister. I think about the elders of your church. Each of these has a responsibility to you and a God-given task to teach His word. Because they have chosen to answer this call, they deserve your honor and respect.

As you look at these verses that command you to respect certain older people in your life, which group is the most difficult for you to respect? Why?

Look at what God says about our parents both in the Old and New Testaments:

Children, obey your parents in the Lord, for this is right. "Honor your father and mother," which is the first commandment with promise: "that it may be well with you and you may live long on the earth." (Ephesians 6:1-3)

Read what Jesus says about honoring our parents as they get older:

He answered and said to them, "Why do you also transgress

27

the commandment of God because of your tradition? For God commanded, saying, 'Honor your father and your mother'; and, 'He who curses father or mother, let him be put to death.' But you say, 'Whoever says to his father or mother, "Whatever profit you might have received from me is a gift to God"–then he need not honor his father or mother.' Thus you have made the commandment of God of no effect by your tradition. Hypocrites! Well did Isaiah prophesy about you, saying: "These people draw near to Me with their mouth, and honor Me with their lips, but their heart is far from Me. And in vain they worship Me, teaching as doctrines the commandments of men.' " (Matthew 15:3-9)

Obviously, God expects us to honor our parents and their role in our lives, and Jesus has a problem with those who don't. Listen to what Paul says about elders and their role in our lives:

Let the elders who rule well be counted worthy of double honor, especially those who labor in the word and doctrine. For the Scripture says, "You shall not muzzle an ox while it treads out the grain," and, "The laborer is worthy of his wages." Do not receive an accusation against an elder except from two or three witnesses. Those who are sinning rebuke in the presence of all, that the rest also may fear. (1 Timothy 5:17-20)

God has appointed these men in His Church, and He expects us to treat them with respect and honor. In 1 Peter 5:5, Peter would tell us as young men to "submit yourselves to your elders." And he went on to say that this should be done in humility. Why? Because this is the attitude God expects of His people towards His people.

The second group of people that the Bible speaks about as being worthy of honor and respect are those who are simply older. In 1 Timothy 5:1-2, Paul says, "Do not rebuke an older man, but exhort him as a father, younger men as brothers, older women as mothers, younger women as sisters, with all purity." We shouldn't view those around us who are older as useless or tired. Instead, we should acknowledge them as wise and cherished. Older people have so much to offer, if we would make it a point to listen and learn from them.

The third group we are instructed to honor is the group of people who are older and have experienced trials. Paul speaks specifically of the widows in 1 Timothy 5:3 and says, "Honor widows who are really widows." In other words, take care of those who have difficulty taking care of themselves.

Honor and Respect

There is one passage in the Old Testament that I want to use to close this discussion. It's found in Leviticus 19:32 and reads, "You shall rise before the gray headed and honor the presence of an old man, and fear your God: I am the Lord." At the beginning of this discussion, I asked you when was the last time you had stood for a lady or for the elderly

> **What is the greatest piece of advice or lesson you have ever learned from someone older? Why did it stick with you?**

when they entered a room. Isn't it interesting that a courtesy like this today might be considered awkward and old-fashioned, and yet, God instilled the practice in the lives of His people thousands of years ago AND coupled it with the idea of fear in Him! The point I'm trying to make is this: Culturally, it might not be required for you to be "over-the-top" in your honor and respect towards those older. Spiritually, it's right in line with what God expects from His people. He knows that loving and respecting Him is demonstrated when we love and respect others.

> **What one older person can you show honor to this week (and continually), and what action will you take to show it?**

It's not hard to be honoring and respectful towards those who are older in your life, but it is something that you will have to do consciously. You will have to decide that older people aren't just old-fashioned and outdated. You will have to decide that they are not stuffy and narrow-minded (although they might be). You will have to decide that in spite of the awkwardness, older people really do have much experience, wisdom, and love to share with you. You will have to act in a way that lifts these people up and lets know that you care. So, honor and respect them! God will bless your life for it!

JDS

Tools for Real Men
Helping to measure up

GOSPEL PREACHERS LIVING HISTORY SERIES

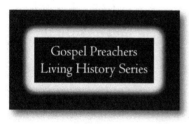

This series is introduced in an effort to preserve the influence of some of the most able preachers of our generation. Each program includes a 30-60 minute interview with the preacher, or with friends and family, conducted by WVBS. Each preacher then delivered one of his favorite sermons. This gives the viewer a chance to become better acquainted with the man, as well as experience what it was like to hear him preach.

video.wvbs.org

SEARCHING FOR TRUTH: ABOUT THE HOUSE OF GOD

Most people in the world live in some kind of house or dwelling. Those houses come in all shapes and sizes, with different floor plans and layouts, and furnished in a lot of different ways. Yet each home is precious and unique to its owner. But have you ever wondered whether or not God owns a house? And if He does, how could we recognize that house if we were to go in search of it today?

searchingfortruth.org

PLEASING GOD IN WORSHIP

This seminar by Dave Miller, Ph.D., provides Bible-based solutions using biblical principles to numerous issues including: May we praise God in whatever way we choose? What about instrumental music, praise teams, etc. with our singing?

video.wvbs.org

30

CHAPTER 6

Defend
the Weak

Frodo: *I can't do this, Sam.*

Sam: *I know. It's all wrong. By rights we shouldn't even be here. But we are. It's like in the great stories, Mr. Frodo. The ones that really mattered. Full of darkness and danger, they were. And sometimes you didn't want to know the end. Because how could the end be happy? How could the world go back to the way it was when so much bad had happened? But in the end, it's only a passing thing, this shadow. Even darkness must pass. A new day will come. And when the sun shines it will shine out the clearer. Those were the stories that stayed with you. That meant something, even if you were too small to understand why. But I think, Mr. Frodo, I do understand. I know now. Folk in those stories had lots of chances of turning back, only they didn't. They kept going. Because they were holding on to something.*

Frodo: *What are we holding onto, Sam?*

Sam: *That there's some good in this world, Mr. Frodo... and it's worth fighting for. - (The Lord of the Rings)*

"For the Lord your God is the God of gods and Lord of lords. He is the great God, the mighty and awesome God, who shows not partiality and cannot be bribed. He ensures that orphans and widows receive justice. He shows love to foreigners living among you and gives them food and clothing. So you, too, must show love...." (Deuteronomy 10:17-19)

When I look back on my life, the years that I regret the most were when I was 13 and 14. Let's face it, 7th and 8th grades are not easy years. And most of us respond to this difficult time by turning into jerks. If we're lucky, we grow out of it. Well, I think I grew out of it, but I don't look back fondly on whom or what I was at the time.

One of the great regrets of my life was the way I treated people when I was in junior high. The great hobby of junior high is to make fun of everything and everyone. Nothing is off limits, and no one is safe. Mercilessly ridiculing someone becomes an art form, and the masters can reduce others to tears. And I was a master. Of course, the reason most junior high kids do this is because they feel that if they make someone else the target of laughter and ridicule, then nobody will notice their mistakes, blunders, and imperfections. Making fun of others becomes a defense mechanism, but it certainly is not the way Christ would act or the way He wants us to act.

Think of a time in your life when you ridiculed someone else. How did that make you feel?

One particularly painful memory from junior high involved a boy in our grade who we will call Mark. Mark was a big, hefty guy who had a really unique way of walking. He kind of walked up on his tip-toes, so he was automatically nicknamed Tippy-Toe. I don't know who the genius was who came up with the nickname, but it stuck fast and hard. Sometimes we even shortened it to Tippy, or even Tip. But wherever Mark went, he was constantly surrounded by those who ridiculed him. And of course, I joined in. Now I don't want you to think I was alone in this or even that I was particularly vicious. I was just going along with the crowd, doing what everyone else did—having a laugh at someone else's expense. But hold on, it gets worse.

Our gym was several hundred yards away from our school building, and on PE days when it wasn't raining, we all walked in a big, loud mob down to the gym. As you can imagine, there was always a lot of laughter and a lot of horseplay. We did ridiculous, painful things to each other. One of the worst things was to take your knee and slam it into another guy's thigh—the big meaty side of his leg. This shot can be excruciatingly painful, especially if you don't see it coming. And this particular day, Mark didn't see it coming. He was walking up ahead of me and a couple of my friends. I uttered those famous last words, "Hey guys, watch this" and took off at a dead sprint. Poor guy never had a chance. I hit him so hard in the thigh with my knee that he immediately went down—and stayed down. As a matter of fact, he rolled around in pain and even started crying. The sight of which would have reduced most people to pity—but not me. Can you guess what I did? I laughed…and laughed. I thought it was the funniest thing I had ever seen. And so did my buddies. As a matter of fact they gave me high-fives for it. And right there for that moment, I was great, because I hurt Mark, and he was the object of laughter.

Here's the problem though. The laughter and high-fives faded away. And what is left is an image of that poor boy lying on the ground crying while I laughed. It's not a memory that sits very well with me. Because here's the thing. Mark didn't come from the kind of home I did. He didn't have the Christian influences I did. He didn't have the friends and popularity I did. He could have used some friendship and compassion. He could have used someone to show him the love of Christ. I should have been that person. But instead, all he got from me was pain and ridicule. I'm hurt by that now and know I should be. I'm hurt because I was strong, confident, and surrounded by friends. I was eventually the captain of the football and basketball teams, voted most likely to succeed, and president of half the clubs at school. I could have made a difference in Mark's life. I could have defended him against ridicule. I could have stood up for him against the crowd. But I became part of the crowd instead.

> Think of a time when you stood up for someone who was weaker and needed help. How did that make you feel?

That is not Real Manhood. That is not being great. Real Men, the kind of men God wants to make us into, are strong, compassionate men who use their strength for the defense of the weak. Because the truth is, God is the God of the underdog. The God who promises to uphold the cause of the poor, the weak, the sick, the disabled, the

33

child, and the unloved. If I ridicule and oppress the weak, the poor, the imperfect, the broken, I am opposing their Great Champion and will myself be crushed to oblivion eventually. If, however, I stand courageously for the poor and weak against the odds and in the face of the ridiculing crowd, I stand with God.

God is the God of the underdog, the weak, the frail, the slave. He destroyed the might of Egypt to release His enslaved people, and He sent a man with a speech impediment to do that. He strengthened Gideon's 300 against an innumerable Midianite host. He gave young David victory over the mighty giant Goliath. He cooled the Babylonian furnace for Shadrach, Meshach, and Abed-Nego when they stood up to a tyrannical king. He shut the mighty lions' mouths to protect his faithful servant Daniel. He championed the cause of Esther against the powerful treachery of Haman. Time and time again the Lord reveals that His mighty arm is on the side of the weak and the oppressed. Consider the following verses:

> *"Defend the cause of the weak and fatherless; maintain the rights of the poor and oppressed." (Psalm 82:3)*

> *"Learn to do good; seek justice, rebuke the oppressor; defend the fatherless, plead for the widow." (Isaiah 1:17)*

God champions the cause of the weak and trampled, and He calls His Men to do the same. Isn't this really what James says pure religion is? To "care for orphans and widows in their trouble," to defend and uphold those who can't do so themselves—this is a noble calling of the man of God (James 1:27).

Help Side

When you are playing in a basketball game, you have to do more than shoot. You've got to learn to play defense as well. You've got to do more than score. You've got to keep the other team from scoring. In doing this, you might learn about "ball-side D" and "help-side D." Ball-side D is what you play when the ball is in your

What is one of the most common reasons teens commit suicide?

34

defensive space. Help-side D is what you play when the ball is in your teammate's space. You back him up. You help him out. If his guy is faster or taller, you bust your tail to get over and pick up some of his slack.

The fact is, all of us need to be playing "help-side." All around us are people who need our help, who need us to pick up some of their slack and get their back. The last thing they need is for us to ridicule and poke fun at them. They need kindness not cruelty. They need reinforcement not ridicule. They need encouragement not discouragement. They need compassion not criticism.

And the truth is, we will become better men for championing the cause of the weak than we will for getting high-fives and laughter for tormenting them. Men of God grow in kindness not cruelty, remembering that Jesus taught that our kindness to others is kindness to Him. So our cruelty to others must be cruelty to Him. We wouldn't think of mocking, bullying, or ridiculing Jesus. But when we treat others that way, we treat Him that way. Jesus' earthly ministry was one of empathy. One of His stated goals was to live among us so that He could mediate for us in Heaven. When Jesus

What do you know about cyber bullying? How have people used modern technology to ridicule others? How can you use it for good?

associated with men though, He didn't hang with the popular, the good-looking, the brilliant, and the athletic. He spent time with the diseased, the discouraged, the demon-possessed, and the downtrodden. Jesus took up the cause of the weak and passed-over, and He calls us to do the very same.

Modern-Day Knights

In the book *Chivalry-The Code of Male Ethics*, the author describes the character of a modern-day knight like this:

Chivalry calls us to be men first in everything we do. It calls us to be strong, compassionate, honest, forthcoming, steadfast, and honorable. It warns us to be prepared, to develop our capabilities with open minds. It points out that the ability to act, to respond, is where manhood comes alive, daring to challenge insurmountable odds, alone if need be, for the good cause. Nature urges us to be protectors, martyrs if need be—which is why we readily follow our comrades onto the battlefield at time of war.

By defending the weak, we take a bold step in following a time-honored code of manly behavior—and promote this code of ethics to other men as well. Heroism inspires the hero in all of us.

Read the story that Nathan told David in 2 Samuel 12:1-4. How does this story relate to what we have learned in this chapter?

Any guy I know, myself included, wants to be a hero to someone: his wife, his children, his girlfriend, his little brother, somebody. One of man's greatest needs is to be admired—to be heroic. But we often seek this admiration by oppressing the weak instead of standing up for them. We use our strengths of personality, humor, athleticism, or popularity to crush instead of champion. Not only is this not heroic, it's downright cowardly. To raise yourself up by pushing someone else down is the true characteristic of a small, weak man.

On the other hand, what we most admire is strength that defends, protects, and serves the weak—not for its own glory, but simply because it's the right thing to do. I mean, none of us wants to be the Joker or the Green Goblin. We want to be Batman or Spiderman or _____ (insert your favorite superhero.) We want to be a hero. This is the heroic strength of our God, the very strength to which He calls us. Jeremiah 22:16 talks about taking up the defense of the poor and needy and asks, "Was not this knowing Me? says the Lord." Defending the weak not only helps us know God, but it also makes us like Him.

"He has shown you, O man, what is good; and what does the Lord require of you but to do justly, to love mercy, and to walk humbly with your God?" (Micah 6:8)

This is a call—not just to know what's right, but to do it. A call to quit bullying and making fun, to stop the ridicule and belittling of those who can't defend themselves. It is a call for a change of your heart and a change of your life. It is a call to empathize with the hurting and step up for them. It is a call for courageous action. And listen, it won't be enough just to stop making fun of, picking on, and bullying the weak. You'll have to stand up for them—against the "cool" people, maybe even against your friends. They might laugh at you. They might make fun of you. You might not get the high-fives. But here's what you will get: self-respect, a clear conscience, gratitude from those you stand for, grudging admiration from those you stand up to, and most importantly, you'll be on God's side. In short, you'll be on your way to becoming a Hero. And we all know the world could use a few more of those.

Discuss some modern examples (such as Oskar Schindler) of those who defended the weak. How can you defend the weak?

SB

Tools for Real Men
Helping to measure up

JUDGMENT DAY: JESUS AS YOUR ATTORNEY

A practicing attorney looks at what the Bible says about Judgment Day. On that day, as in trials here on earth, we can have a defense – a lawyer who is our perfect Advocate. He knows the Judge, understands the prosecutor, and died to set us free. Study with Gary Massey on this important subject.

video.wvbs.org

EVIL, PAIN AND SUFFERING

Where is God when I hurt? Why do innocent people suffer? How could a loving God let this happen? Millions of people have searched for answers to the questions of why there is Evil, Pain and Suffering in the world. If you are one of them, you need to see this video. While many use the Problem of Evil as an argument against God's existence, recognizing the contrast between what is good and what is evil points to the existence of God as a moral lawgiver.

evilpainandsuffering.com

A WOMAN'S CHOICE

Unplanned pregnancy? Don't know what to do? What are your choices? 'A Woman's Choice' is an engaging video designed to help women who find themselves with an unexpected pregnancy and pressed with decisions of what to do.

pregnancydecisions.org

A LIFE OF ACTION | SERMON BY KYLE BUTT

It is troubling to hear of situations where wrongdoing occurs and bystanders fail to do anything to help, especially when it involves the well-being of another person. Sadly, a "do nothing" mentality is often embraced by society as being politically correct and socially

acceptable, even when considering Christianity. In this video, Kyle Butt challenges those who understand Christianity as a list of things that should not be done by calling to attention our true purpose as followers of Christ: seeking to glorify God by using our talents and resources in proactively meeting the needs of others and engaging in good works, according to His will.

video.wvbs.org

CHAPTER 7

How To Get Along With Your Parents

"Fathers are to sons what blacksmiths are to swords. It is the job of the blacksmith not only to make a sword but also to maintain its edge of sharpness. It is the job of the father to keep his son sharp and save him from the dullness of foolishness. He gives his son that sharp edge through discipline." (Steve Farrar)

"Honor your father, as the Lord commanded you...." (Deuteronomy 5:16)

Admirable, trustworthy, compassionate, loving, understanding, committed, spiritual...AWESOME!?! I can honestly tell you that these words were not in my vocabulary when I was a teenager trying to describe my parents. Words like mean, impatient, harsh, stupid, ridiculous, etc. were the words that most often dripped off my tongue in disgust about something my parents had done to me.

What changed? I guess time did...I grew up. I learned to realize the value of my parents in my life. As you read this chapter, my prayer for you is that you will one day have the same type of relationship with your parents that I do—honoring and loving. But that doesn't help you right now, does it? You may even be asking, "How does praying for something in the future, help me in the middle of my difficulty now?"

The Difficulty

Let's face it, being a teenager is just plain difficult! There are hundreds of books out there for parents who are having difficulty with their teenagers, but what about books for teenagers who are having difficulty with their parents? Right now, you're in the middle of "There's no hope for my parents!" and "How embarrassing!" At this very moment, you may be dwelling on how unfair and unjust they are to you. Right now, you can't wait until the day you get to leave home. You may be thinking to yourself, "They just don't understand," or "I wish they'd let me grow up," or even, "I wish they'd just leave me alone." Let's face it, parents just don't get it! And I remember having these same thoughts and feelings when I was a teenager.

What are some of the most difficult challenges you have with your parents?

And I'm not just saying that either…I remember being 15 minutes late for curfew one night. You'd have thought I'd died—actually my mom thought I did. By the time I got home—only 15 minutes late—she was already driving around town looking for me in a ditch. So, I got grounded. I remember how dad would come home and start in on me for not doing my chores…I thought he was being such a jerk! Mom would ground me for lying; dad would give me more work for hitting my siblings; mom would send me to my room for smarting off; dad would take my cars keys because of my irresponsibility. He even fired me from working with him at the farm one day. All in all, my parents were just as unfair as yours are right now, because "they just didn't understand!"

What aspects of parental conflict do you think are your fault? What aspects of parental conflict do you think might be your parents' fault?

So, the real challenge we're faced with is, "How can I learn to live with them when they don't seem to understand?" There's no doubt that every teen throughout history has asked this same question. The truth is that we all struggle with our parents. I guess that's the way our culture says it's supposed to be. But guess what, it doesn't have to be that way.

You see, your relationship with your parents is not about having to "put up with them" until you're out of the house. It's not about having to love them just because they're your parents. It's about having a deep down love and respect for them because of who they are and what they are doing for you—even when you don't like their decisions or actions all the time. And if they're not being who they ought to be and doing what they ought to do as godly parents, then it's about your love and respect for them because of who you are as a son of God. It's all about a journey, a process that will lead you into an honoring and loving relationship, both now and in the future.

Now, I'll go ahead and admit that this is not going to be an easy journey. As a matter of fact, it may be the most difficult journey you've taken up to this point in your life— your learning to love, honor, and even submit to your parents' authority. But it's not always easy for your parents to be your parents either. Look, I believe in every man's right to life, liberty, and the pursuit of happiness as much as the next guy. And I know that it often seems like your parents are trying to strip you of all of these. But contrary to popular belief, they don't enjoy grounding you or saying "no", and they certainly don't look forward to the awkward lectures about the "birds and the bees." They don't like arguing with you all the time about your maturity and how grown up you are.

Why do you think God instructs children to honor their parents (Ephesians 6:1-2)?

Here's my theory: We are in a big hurry to grow up and prove to the world that we really are grown men. Our parents, on the other hand, continue to view us as the little boy who needed daddy to teach him how to ride his bike and tie his shoe. We claim maturity; they see inexperience. We think we can do it all; they know we can't. The war wages on between the discipline and teaching our parents are trying to give us and the independence and maturity we believe we deserve. Does that sound about right? Are they really that mistaken all the time? Maybe they know a little bit more about life, love, and happiness than we think they do. And maybe they are doing all they can to instill within us the knowledge and wisdom we need to pursue these things in a godly way.

We are in a big hurry to grow up and prove to the world that we really are grown men.

The Design

God gets it right, and He got it right when He designed the family— one father, one mother, and children. The man is the head of the family, and he is to love his wife. The woman is to love and respect her husband. Their job is to procreate—have lots of children to boss around however

41

they want. Of course, it's not quite as bad as we like to make it sound. As a matter of fact, God's design for the family is the perfect vehicle for the training and instruction of children. Maybe your parents understand God's will and are trying very hard to abide by it—no matter how bad it seems. Unfortunately, not all parents are trying to abide by God's will, but that doesn't mean you should give up on the journey.

In Ephesians 6:1-4, God tells children to "obey your parents," and "honor your father and mother." He also tells fathers, "do not provoke your children to anger, but bring them up in the discipline and instruction of the Lord." In other words, fathers are to instruct their children (you) in the ways of life, and more importantly, in the way of the Lord. They are charged to do this in gentleness and love, so that they do not cause anger or discontentment within the child. They are not to be overbearing or degrading so as not to destroy or discourage the child. Not so bad is it? But you may be thinking right now about all the times your dad has made you angry, either by things he's said or done that hurt you. Remember this, he's only a dad, and dads make mistakes. If he is doing his very best to instruct you in the ways of the Lord, and I pray he is, then he probably had no intentions of causing you harm. Nevertheless, he is still commanded to "discipline" and "instruct" you. And yes, sometimes it will be difficult.

The Discipline

So let's talk about the ideas of "discipline" and "instruction." Your father's obligation to you is to teach you about life—a spiritual life in relationship to the Father, Son, and Holy Spirit, and a social life of interaction and success. Your obligation to your parents is to learn from them and obey them. Remember that Jesus in Luke 2:52 "grew in wisdom, stature, and favor with God and man." He knew that He had to learn from them, and that meant that He also had to "honor and obey" their instruction for Him. Growth is a process of maturity that must include learning. If the Son of God needed to go through this process, how much more do we, as flailing adolescents, need this process?

Why do you think God says that all loving fathers discipline their children (Hebrews 12:5-11)?

So what is your father supposed to be teaching you? The wisest man the world has ever seen, Solomon, said in Proverbs 1:7 that "the fear of the Lord is the beginning of wisdom." Another way to think about the meaning of this verse is to replace the word "fear" with "reverence" or "respect" (a deep and humble awe). In other words, your father's job (Ephesians 6 coupled with Proverbs 1) is to teach you how to live a life that is in constant reverence of Who God is and what God says in His word. Jesus reiterated this concept in a different way by restating the 1st and greatest command: "Love the Lord your God with all your heart, soul, mind, and strength" (Matthew 22:37). And of course, He would go on to state the 2nd greatest command: "Love your neighbor as yourself" (Matthew 22:39).

If there is one thing lacking in this world, it is a general love and respect for both God and fellow man. "God" is often little more than a name that is taken in vain during times of surprise or disdain. He has been cast aside as an inconvenience. People are disregarded as people, but referred to as objects, jokes, or inconveniences. Very few take up for the elderly, weak, or different. Students disrespect teachers. Children disobey parents. Employers are even ignored in the workplace, because so many push the envelope of cheating company resources and time. After reading this chapter, I challenge you to observe your peers in school and notice how little respect there is even among your group of friends.

Kind of disgusting isn't it…to think that so much degradation has taken place in our society!? This is why, hopefully, your parents are teaching you simple things like manners and courtesy, honesty and integrity. This is why they harp on your behavior so much and bust you for lying. This is why they urge you to behave in worship and Bible class. They don't want you to grow up to be an adult full of disregard for God and others. So pay attention to these things. I guarantee it will pay off for you later. You, in turn, will be respected and admired by others, and you will have developed a love and relationship with God that is all-sustaining.

> **What aspects of discipline show love? Why would it be unloving to fail to discipline a child?**

The Decision

So are you fed up with this chapter yet? Are you rolling your eyes, because all this chapter is about is your attitude and responsibility? Are you thinking to yourself, "What am I supposed to do with all this talk about my attitude and responsibility?" Especially when it's your parents who have the problem, right? We can look at our situation as sons from this point forward in one of two ways: We can either be resentful towards God and our parents, because we are called to act a certain way. Or we can be thankful that we have a God who understands our need for maturity and has provided it through parents (or parental figures) who love us.

Did you know this? In the Old Testament, if a boy dishonored his parents in a shameful way, they were instructed to stone him (Deuteronomy 21:18-21). If he didn't die by the stone, he at least suffered by the rod...literally...not a spanking, but a beating! I wonder how many young men would be lost to the world, our country, your school, or even your congregation if this Biblical law were still enforced. Would you deserve stoning based on your attitude towards your parents? Can you imagine the resentment the Hebrew boys might have held toward their dads when they heard, "Clean your room...or ELSE!"? I don't think any of us really want to resent our parents for the rest of our lives.

Let's look at attitude-option number two. God gives us a great look at the father-son relationship in Hebrews 12:5-9 by paralleling it with His love for us and the discipline we absolutely must have in these relationships. Phrases like "those He loves," "accepts as a son," and "true sons" are given for us to understand one thing in our relationships with our fathers—both heavenly and earthly. We are disciplined, because we are loved! Period. What a profound simple truth for us to remember. Our heavenly Father loves us, so He disciplines us as we need it—never fun. Our dads love us, so they discipline us as we need—never fun. God is perfect in His discipline. Our fathers are trying! Both are motivated by love! This second attitude is a little harder for us to swallow and live by, but it could revolutionize our outlook toward our parents, if we would learn to adopt it.

> Have you seen young people who were not disciplined? Why do you think teens who are not disciplined, deep down, want boundaries and discipline?

The Destination

They say that Rome wasn't built in a day...come on, the roads to Rome weren't even built in a day. Your relationship with your parents, if hurting, won't get better over night. But if you are willing to work at it, you can certainly cover a lot of distance in this new journey. Oh, and "work" is the key-word here, because you can't change anyone's attitude but your own. Your parents will react in response to the changes you make in your life. Just be patient and persistent.

1. Check your map. You know where you want to go, but now you need to know how to get there. Stay in touch with God's word. You don't always have to go to the "parent-child" passages to see the path. You will need to see what God says about your behavior, thoughts, and attitudes in general to get where you need to go (2 Timothy 3:16-17).

2. Check your direction. It's pointless to know the way to go but not change your direction when you're off-course. What behaviors, thoughts, and attitudes do you need to change so that you will be more pleasant and godly in your relationships? (James 1:22-25).

3. Check your progress. Do your best to be honest and open in your relationship with God and your parents. Communication is the key on both levels. With your parents, it may only be one-sided for a time, but that doesn't mean you won't see glimpses of progress in their reaction towards you. God will work with you through this process! (Philippians 4:4-7).

Above all, remember who you are! Nothing your parents do, no matter how mad or frustrated they make you, can take away from the fact that you are a son of God. If you are striving to be God's child, first and foremost, in everything you do, then you will undoubtedly be the son your parents are training you to be in honor and obedience. Because of your relationship with Him, honor and obedience will always characterize your relationship with them. God speed you on your journey!

JDS

Tools for Real Men
Helping to measure up

RECEIVING CORRECTION | SERMON BY KYLE BUTT

In this video, Kyle Butt discusses an essential attribute a person must possess in order to achieve life in heaven: a proper attitude and reception of correction. Kyle presents a very simple and direct lesson on the importance of receiving correction, as emphasized by the Lord in the wisdom literature of Scripture.

video.wvbs.org

THE TRUTH ABOUT LYING

"The Truth About... Lying" covers the controversial topic of lying. Should we lie to try and benefit ourselves or others? Sooner or later, most of us find ourselves facing moral, social, and ethical situations that command our attention. These situations can affect our family, friends, neighbors or others.

video.wvbs.org

LOST | SERMONS BY MIKE VESTAL

The program, Lost, focuses on the parable told by Jesus in Luke chapter 15. Mike Vestal details eight perspectives found in this story with sermons titled: (1) Who Cares? (2) Happy Days, (3) Rebels Without A Cause, (4) Prone To Wander, (5) The Turning Point, (6) A Father's Heart, (7) A Glimpse Of God, and (8) Staying Home.

video.wvbs.org

CHAPTER 8

Watch Your Mouth

"We have two ears and one tongue so that we would listen more and talk less." (Diogenes)

"For by your words you will be justified, and by your words you will be condemned." (Matthew 12:37)

As I begin this chapter, I am sitting at a camp compound in Sarchi, Costa Rica in Central America. Our goal is to plant preacher camps for young men in all of Central America and in parts of South America. And let me tell you, the experience is awesome! Aside from meeting all kinds of amazing people in the Lord's Church, I also get to see some amazing parts of creation. This morning as I walked out the door of my cabin, I had the opportunity to take in the beauty of God's creation in the form of a simple little stream. It is crystal clear and fast flowing. You can see every smooth rock in its bed, and little pink flowers cover its banks on either side. Every few feet a tree grows out of the flowers and stands watch over the water's perfection. As clear and pure as the water seems to be, there are certain impurities that we gringos (US natives that have no clue how to speak Spanish outside of what we have learned from Taco Bell) have to be very careful not to ingest. The impurities are microscopic bacteria waiting to wreak havoc on an innocent, weak digestive system. What's the big deal? God created this stream to be beautiful and useful, but it is tainted by filth that is very harmful and very destructive to the unsuspecting.

> Think of a time when you used your words to hurt another person. Why do you think you can remember that so well?

Unfortunately, it is often the very same with our mouths. God made our mouths with the intention that we would use them for beautiful words and the joy of tasting. Instead, we often use them for harm and destruction. How can such harmful impurities be found in such a beautiful place? Well, in the case of our mouths, it simply should not be! But let's be real for a moment...from the time we were able to speak, we have struggled with the right things to say. Our parents would tell us to do something, and we would throw out the word "NO!" in disobedience. We went to kindergarten and began to hear and repeat words that shouldn't be known by five-year-olds. We got to junior high, and we started hearing sexual slang and cursing in the locker room and at the lunch table. And now you're in high school. Has it gotten any easier for you to control your tongue?

As we think about controlling our mouths in the next few pages of this chapter, I want to challenge you with three simple truths. These may not be new to you, because these truths come straight from God's word. I hope that you will be reminded, however, of the power of the tongue. And I hope that you will be challenged and encouraged to cleanse the impurities of your tongue. Most importantly, my prayer is that you will give God the control of your tongue, so that He can use it in His will.

Truth #1: The Tongue Is a Fire

Have you ever watched news footage of the West Coast wild fires that break out each summer? They are always out of control and devastating to everything in their path. They scar, burn, and destroy miles of forest and fields. People are left without homes. It doesn't matter how many choppers and firefighters they have on site trying to put the fires out, they just keep burning...out of control and with no remorse. This is exactly how the tongue is described in James 3:5-6. It is a fire that is out of control and cannot be tamed. As a matter of fact, James goes on to say in verse 7 that every kind of animal on the Earth has been tamed, or subdued, by man, and yet, the tongue continues to remain out of control.

I want you to think about the significance of the idea of taming for a moment. If you have ever been to Sea World, you've watched people swim with killer whales and do flips off their massive snouts. If you have ever been to the Dixie Stampede in Pigeon Forge, TN, you've seen people ride ostriches like horses. I've seen

From your experiences, what are the motives behind hurtful words? Why do you sometimes hurt others? Why do they sometimes hurt you?

a woman actually dance with a horse in an arena (I know it sounds weird, but it was pretty amazing to see). I've heard birds talk; I've seen men wrestle alligators; I watched a man on Stan Lee's Super-Humans swim with sharks without a cage; I've seen pictures of ancient Indian carvings in which men were riding dinosaurs. The point is that, throughout our world's history, man has been able to figure out how to have control over and subdue most every creature on this planet. And yet, every day we struggle with our tongues. We "slip up" and spit out bad words. We destroy people's confidence with hurtful and mean words. We crush people with sharp and cutting words of discontent. We turn girls and women (many of whom are our Christian sisters) into objects by the way we describe them with vulgar, sexual words. We undermine our parents, teachers, bosses, and coaches with disrespectful words.

The problem with this type of behavior is that it is never justifiable. God will not accept the excuse that we "slipped." He doesn't overlook sinful words because you snapped because of exhaustion when someone was bothering you after a long day. God doesn't care if most of the time you listen to your parents, but you only talk back at them occasionally in front of others. God doesn't care about our excuses. Why?

God has called us to a higher calling. If we are Christians, then we are called to control who we are. Therefore, we have no right to speak harshly or wrongly in any way to other people. As a matter-of-fact, if we look back at James 3, we see that God even calls into question our love for Him if we are unable to control our speech toward others. James writes in verses 9-10, "With it [our tongue] we bless our God and Father, and with it we curse men, who

Read Luke 6:45. What do you think Jesus is trying to tell us in this verse?

49

have been made in the similitude of God. Out of the same mouth proceed blessing and cursing. My brethren, these things ought not to be so." Simply put, we have no right to call ourselves Christians if we do not control our tongues. So what does it mean to struggle with the control of our tongues?

Truth #2: The Fire Must Always Be Fought

Unfortunately, bad language and speech are not "little" bad habits or growing pains that just go away. As a matter-of-fact, we alluded earlier to the idea that struggling with our speech only becomes more and more difficult as we grow up surrounded by a dark world. It is a struggle we must face on a daily basis in order to be successful.

Paul says in Ephesians 5:1-4:

Therefore be imitators of God as dear children. And walk in love, as Christ also has loved us and given Himself for us, an offering and a sacrifice to God for a sweet-smelling aroma. But fornication and all uncleanness or covetousness, let it not even be named among you, as is fitting for saints; neither filthiness, nor foolish talking, nor coarse jesting, which are not fitting, but rather giving of thanks.

Discuss the various sins of the tongue. In contrast, discuss the various ways the tongue can be used for good.

Did you notice that Paul grouped our speech in the same category as fornication and covetousness? Pretty serious stuff, right? Here's why: Purity is what we should be striving for in our daily lives, and I think that most of us would agree with that. But most of us still struggle with our tongues. Yet some of us dismiss the need to struggle with our tongues. Paul is making sure that we understand that there is no difference in sexual impurity or speech impurity when it comes to our love for God. You can't be pure in one area, allow the other area to be polluted, and still claim that you love God.

Paul goes on to say in Ephesians 5:8-12, "You were once darkness, but now you are light in the Lord. Walk as children of light (for the fruit of the Spirit is in all goodness, righteousness, and truth), finding out what is acceptable to the Lord. And have no fellowship with the unfruitful works of darkness, but rather expose them." Simply put, for you to control your tongue, you must make a conscious decision to refrain from speaking evil things. This means that you don't allow words to just "slip out" of your mouth as often as they did the day before. You don't back-talk your parents or disrespect people of authority in your life. You don't join in with the slang and joking and perversion at school. Instead, you make sure that people know where you stand in your love for God. You won't speak in an ungodly way any longer, and you won't stand by and listen to others do the same. That's what it means to struggle with your tongue.

Truth #3: The Fire Must Be Tamed

Forest fires rage out of control, but bonfires are awesome to behold. What's the difference? Obviously, in spite of the fact that they are both fires, one has been placed within a boundary and is constantly monitored. Instead of now being destructive and all consuming, a bonfire can be used for good things like safety, warmth, and cooking. In extreme cases, bonfires or campfires can even save people's lives. It's the same with our tongues.

> It has been said: "Sticks and stones may break my bones, but words can never hurt me." Why is that statement false?

No longer are we using our tongues to destroy, but now we are using our tongues to bring people to the safety of salvation. We are warming people's hearts with words of encouragement. We are feeding people with our love for the truth.

Look at these verses on your own for a moment and notice what God says about taking away the evil of our tongues and replacing it with good.

-Psalm 34:11-14

-Psalm 39:1-5

-Psalm 51:13-15

-Proverbs 12:17-19

-Proverbs 18:20-21

-Isaiah 50:4

-Jeremiah 1:7-9

-Matthew 15:10-20

I hope you took the time to really pay attention to these verses—of course, there are so many more that we could look at in the Bible. But, there is one scene in the Bible that I left out of that list. It's found in Isaiah 6.

In Isaiah 6, the prophet finds himself before God in His very throne room, and Isaiah is afraid to have seen God and spoken to Him with unclean lips. One of the seraphs (a heavenly being) flies to Isaiah with a hot coal from the fire and touches his lips with it. From this point forward, God wants Isaiah to understand that His filth is atoned, but now He has been given a message for God's people.

This is the lesson I want to leave with you in our discussion of the third truth: When you strive to take away the sinful talk of your mouth, make sure you replace it with the message of love and joy and hope that only God can give us. In Ephesians 4:29, Paul says:

Let no corrupt word proceed out of your mouth, but what is good for necessary edification, that it may impart grace to the hearers. And do not grieve the Holy Spirit of God, by whom you were sealed for the day of redemption. Let all bitterness, wrath, anger, clamor, and evil speaking be put away from you, with all malice. And be kind to one another, tenderhearted, forgiving one another, even as God in Christ forgave you.

Did you notice the significant words in this passage—good, edification, grace to the hearers, kind, tenderhearted? All people like to be treated in these ways! If you are going to tame your tongue, you must replace bad speech with the speech of God, and you must rely on His power to succeed.

Just like Isaiah, I want you to imagine what you could do for a lost world when you are willing to put away the sinful nature of the mouth and take up the message of God. No longer will your tongue of fire control you, but you will embrace the fire of God's word in such a way that your tongue will become beneficial to God's kingdom.

Why do you believe that James said that if a man does not bridle his tongue then his religion is useless (James 1:26)?

JDS

Tools for Real Men
Helping to measure up

HYPOCRITE!

"HYPOCRITE!"
-Jesus Christ

Are you tired of hypocritical religious leaders? Are you tired of people not practicing what they preach? Good, Jesus was tired of that attitude, too. In the Sermon on the Mount, Jesus said that our righteousness must exceed what the Pharisees and Jewish leaders of his day were demonstrating. Jesus taught against hypocrisy on a multitude of issues. Join Eddie Parrish in this short video as he expounds on the meaningful lessons from the Sermon on the Mount.

video.wvbs.org

THE TRUTH ABOUT LYING (PART 1)

"The Truth About Lying" covers the controversial topic of lying. Should we lie to try and benefit ourselves or others? Sooner or later, most of us find ourselves facing moral, social, and ethical situations that command our attention.

video.wvbs.org

THE TRUTH ABOUT LYING (PART 2)

"The Truth About Lying" covers the temptations for you to tell a lie. These situations can affect our family, friends, neighbors or others. In an easy-to-understand manner, Don Blackwell presents a compelling and informative answer from a biblical and practical standpoint.

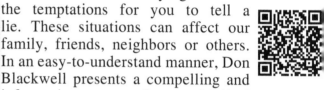

video.wvbs.org

DOES PRAYER WORK? | SEARCH PRAYER

Have you ever wondered, "Does prayer work?" The Bible instructs Christians to "pray without ceasing" (1 Thessalonians 5:17). God listens to our prayers and knows what is best for our lives. So the answer is, " Yes prayer works!" God's power, wisdom, and will for our lives guides how He will answer our requests. Join Kevin Rutherford as he looks at what the Bible says about effective prayers.

video.wvbs.org

CHAPTER 9

The Call To Sexual Purity

"Character is what a man is in the dark." (Dwight L. Moody)

"This is the will of God, your sanctification: that you should abstain from sexual immorality; that each of you should know how to possess his own vessel in sanctification and honor...." (1 Thessalonians 4:3-4)

The ancient Greeks had a legend about a great hero named Achilles. He was half mortal and half god, a demi-god, and he was pretty much indestructible. As an infant, his mother carried him to the Underworld and dipped him in the River Styx. This particular pagan baptism insured that Achilles could never be injured or killed. There was only one problem: when the person doing the dipping dunked baby Achilles in the water, she held him by the heel. Every part of Achilles was mystically protected—EXCEPT the heel that was not dipped. (Did you know that you have an Achilles tendon? Guess where it is.) Achilles' exploits during the siege of Troy were epic, literally. But Achilles' story, and life, come to a predictable end when the biggest wimp in the whole story accidentally shoots Achilles—you guessed it—in the heel. The end. The bigger they are the harder they fall.

Even the strongest Men have weaknesses. The world is trying to find them. The Devil is trying to find them. If there is anything that is a greater challenge to Men today than sexual purity, I sure don't know what it is.

> **What do you think your primary weakness is? What can you do to work on it?**

I was never very tempted to curse and use bad language. I didn't see the point. In fact, in my whole life I think only one person has ever heard one curse word come out of my mouth. I knew drugs and alcohol were stupid and dangerous. I never much wanted to break the law by vandalizing or stealing anything. Of course, all of those things can be tempting. But personally, none of them tempted me much. What I had the most problem with was sexual temptation. I imagine I'm not the only one.

This chapter is going to be the first of two chapters that are a frank and honest discussion about sexual temptation and the Man of God.

Let's start with the basics:

1) Sex is a beautiful, God-designed act intended for mutual enjoyment and fulfillment of the physical, emotional, and psychological needs of a husband and wife. Sex is a good thing.

2) The beauty of sex is tarnished and destroyed when men and women forsake God's plan. It becomes a dirty, shameful, almost animal act when practiced in a worldly context and sinful situation. There is no good that can come from sinful sex. Those same physical, emotional, and psychological needs that godly sex fulfills are left unfulfilled; and individuals are left hurting, unsatisfied, and often perverted. God did not make sex sinful, bad, dirty, and shameful. The World did.

Why do you think some religious people in the past portrayed virtually all sex as dirty or sinful?

3) The Bible—God's owner's manual for the human life and body—has a lot to say about sex. Not just the right and wrong of it either. But the practical, everyday side of our sexuality. I hear a lot of people say, "Well, the Bible doesn't say anything about that." Chances are it does. We are admitting our ignorance when we argue otherwise. Sometimes, however, we don't know the meaning of the words the Bible uses to deal with something that may be very relevant to our particular situation.

Why do you think the Bible says so much about sex?

Let's call this next section then…

Big Bible Words About Sex and What They Mean to Me

I'm going to make sure these definitions are practical and easy to use. It won't help anybody if the definition is as hard to read as the word. These are not the fullest definitions, but they are at least workable for our study. There is also a verse included with each definition so you can see how the word is used in a Biblical context.

> **a. Adultery**—the sin committed when a married person has sex with someone other than his/her spouse. A marriage is involved. If two people who are not married or who have never been married have sex, it is not adultery. (Exodus 20:14—"You shall not commit **adultery**.")
>
> **b. Fornication**—a word with broad meanings, sometimes translated "sexual immorality," the sin committed when two people who are not married have sex. Fornication is from the same Greek root (porneia) as the English word pornography. (1 Corinthians 6:18—"he who commits **fornication** sins against his own body.")
>
> **c. Lust**—a strong desire to do or have something sinful. Sexual sin always begins with lust. (James 1:14—"Each one is tempted when he is drawn away by his own **lusts**….")

57

d. Lasciviousness—shameless actions showing no restraint, self-control, or desire to do what is right. Used to describe the actions of wicked men in 2 Peter 2:18.

e. Lewd—filthy or dirty, dishonorable. (Ezekiel 24:13—"In your filthiness is **lewdness**. Because I have cleansed you, and you were not cleansed, you will not be cleansed of your filthiness anymore, till I have caused My fury to rest upon you.")

> **What are some things in our society that would be lewd or lascivious?**

f. Sanctify—God's people are cleansed and set apart from the World for His service. The Bible concept of holiness has the same meaning. (1 Corinthians 6:10-11—"Do not be deceived. Neither fornicators, nor idolaters, nor adulterers, nor homosexuals, nor sodomites...will inherit the kingdom of God. And such were some of you. But you were washed, but you were sanctified, but you were justified in the name of the Lord Jesus and by the Spirit of our God.")

g. Defile—to make common or unclean. It is the opposite of the word sanctify. (1 Corinthians 3:17—"If anyone defiles the temple of God, God will destroy him. For the temple of God is holy, which temple you are.")

h. Pure—clean, not contaminated. (1 Timothy 5:22—"Keep yourself pure.")

These aren't the only biblical words on the subject, but they are the main ones and should give us a good Bible vocabulary for our discussion. But first we need to make one important point...

You Are Not an Animal

Open up any biology book in school, look up evolution, and you'll find it—that chart that shows how a one-celled amoeba turned into a multi-celled organism, then into a frog-like lizard, which crawled out of a sludgy swamp to turn into a groundhog-sized deer/goat/lizard/cat/dog, that became a funny looking monkey-type thing, that grew and grew, shaved, developed better posture and is now modern man. Hey they've got pictures! It's in the science book! It must be true! And the anthropological significance? Man is nothing more than a clean, smart animal.

This is the world's basis for teaching about sex: "We are nothing more than animals; and the sex act does nothing more than satisfy a natural and undeniable appetite rooted in the species' evolutionary mandate to reproduce; therefore, one can engage in sexual activity with the casualness of eating, drinking or sleeping." Sexual slang and cultural vocabulary depict sex as an animal act with no deep meaning, significance, or consequences. Ever heard anything like this? "I'm into having sex. I'm not into making love." Songs and music videos often portray barely clothed people acting like sexually-crazed animals and being proud of it. The "animalization" of man through evolutionary teaching has warped and degraded mankind's understanding of sexuality.

What has the false theory of evolution done to our culture's view of sex?

Made in God's Image

The Bible teaches the opposite. Mankind is not only higher than animals—smarter, sophisticated, and cultured—but he is altogether different than animals. Before God created Man, He made a divine proposal. "Let Us make man in Our image." Being made in the image of God has several consequences. First, we have the ability to choose between right and wrong. We make decisions based on moral considerations. Everybody does. People are quick to point out, "Hey that's not right," or "That's not fair." Rightness or wrongness is a concept animals do not know.

Second, because we have been made spiritual beings in the image of God, the moral choices that we make have serious physical, emotional, psychological, and eternal consequences. Man has to answer for his actions before God in judgment. Animals do not. Third, being made in the image of God means that Man is capable of love. Human beings' ability to communicate and consider higher concepts means that we are able to know and comprehend deeper and stronger feelings than animals. We feel guilt, shame, anxiety, rejection, compassion, friendship, hate, love, and a wide spectrum of other feelings. Of course, we have all been amazed at the seeming emotional consciousness that some animals demonstrate, but these feelings have nowhere near the depth, complexity, intensity, or duration of human feelings.

Because of all these reasons, Man, made in the image of God, is special—unique in all Creation. And this "specialness" is important in our present discussion about sexuality. Human sex is entirely different from animal sex because of the reasons discussed above. But consider this wonderful fact: Human beings are mammals that mate face-to-face. (Whoa guy! What's this book rated anyway? If you don't know the particulars of human sexuality, you probably need some more information before you can evaluate that last statement. Unfortunately, this is not the ideal forum for such a lesson, but you need some good Christian information on the subject. I would suggest you ask your parents. Uncomfortable? You bet! But very important. They need to teach it, and you need to learn it.) This interesting anatomical fact is hardly a coincidence. It's what makes human sexual intercourse one of the most beautiful, intimate, and personal acts in the world. Humans have the ability to mate eye-to-eye, mouth-to-mouth, heart-to-heart. Sexual intercourse is a blessing shared between a man and woman. Animal sex, on the other hand, is selfish. It cares nothing about the other individual. It seeks instant, primal, self-gratification and the perpetuation of the species instead of the emotional bonding that should occur when a man and woman make love. Human sexuality is mysterious and deeply emotional. Animal sexuality is not.

How many lives have been ruined, because people were careless about human sexuality? How many poor girls are prostitutes, because they didn't understand the tragic consequences of abused sexuality? How many men have a shallow, selfish, or perverted sexuality, because they were never taught to appreciate or understand the depth and complexity of human sex?

What famous athletes or politicians can you list whose lives were ruined because of sex?

The most famous psychologist who ever lived, Sigmund Freud, "the father of psycho analysis," argued that sexuality is the single most pervasive factor in our identity. And while I might not go that far, I do want you to realize that your sexuality must be treated, cherished, nourished, and protected as the wonderful gift from God that it is.

SB

Tools for Real Men
Helping to measure up

ABSTINENCE OR SEX: YOUR CHOICE

The material presented by Kyle Butt is designed for churches to use in combating the lies about sex that are perpetrated on our young people through the media, schools and friends. The seminar teaches God's plan of sexual abstinence before marriage. This material is very frank and explicit regarding the various kinds of sexual diseases that can result from participation in those activities.

abstinenceorsex.com

THE TRUTH ABOUT MODESTY

"The Truth About... Modesty" covers the important topic of modesty. Can Christians wear anything a store sells? Do cultural norms change a Christian's perspective? Sooner or later, most of us find ourselves facing moral, social, and ethical situations that command our attention. These situations can affect our family, friends, neighbors or others. In an easy-to-understand manner, Don Blackwell presents a compelling and informative answer from a biblical and practical standpoint.

video.wvbs.org

THE TRUTH ABOUT DRINKING

"The Truth About... Drinking" covers the controversial topic of Social Drinking. Can Christians engage in social drinking? What constitutes drunkenness? Sooner or later, most of us find ourselves facing moral, social, and ethical situations that command our attention. These situations can affect our family, friends, neighbors or others. In an easy-to-understand manner, Don Blackwell presents a compelling and informative answer from a biblical and practical standpoint.

video.wvbs.org

CHAPTER 10

The Battle Against Sexual Temptation

"Every life is a march from innocence, through temptation, to virtue or vice." (Lyman Abbot)

"Flee also youthful lusts; but pursue righteousness, faith, love, peace with those who call on the Lord out of a pure heart." (2 Timothy 2:22)

I'm sitting in my bedroom right now with my laptop out writing a chapter on overcoming sexual temptation. Just before I began writing, I got a message from Mariana on my Skype account. Skype is a program that allows you to use the camera on your computer to send a live video stream instantly to your friends all across the world. I set up an account to keep in touch with one of my roommates from college. It is amazing to be hours away from each other, yet still be able to sit at a computer and talk just like we were in the same room. The irony of tonight's writing is that I have never gotten a message from any other person on Skype but Chad, my old roommate…until tonight at about 11:15. Tonight, the mysterious Mariana, just minutes before I started typing, wrote me the following message that I quote for you word-for-word:

> *Right now I am just looking to have some…fun. I didn't think I would ever get what I wanted without going through that relationship process. I found this personal matching site and ever since I have had all the erotic personal encounters I can handle! Anonymous email, chat, & instant message with others. Meet them anytime you want. There are thousands of curious swingers in your area. Check it out, see if you like it. You don't need to pay to play in this community. Press here if you want to get wild.*

My wife is in the other room watching a movie and I have wireless Internet access. I know how to erase the history on this computer, and

I'm pretty sure nobody will disturb me for at least 30 minutes, maybe an hour. I could easily click on Mariana's site and start the process of scheduling "all the erotic personal encounters I can handle." The truth is, you young men reading this book could do the same just about any time you want. Many of you have Internet access on your phones, for crying out loud. You can sneak off by yourself on a regular basis and check out the sensuous bodies of naked women whenever you please. You know as well as I do that you can find whatever size you want, in whatever pose, at pretty much whatever time you want. But do you know what? I'm barely even tempted (I'm not going to say not at all, but barely) to click that site. But let me give you the main reason, which you already know, why millions of guys do click Mariana's site.

Why do you think so many men are tripped up by sexual temptation?

Sex is Fun and Exciting...but Often Toxic

There is absolutely, positively no question that the act of sex, or looking at pornography and "helping yourself out" is physically enjoyable. If it weren't, there wouldn't be any temptation to do it. I mean, come on, if it felt like stepping on a rusty nail, we would all avoid it like the plague. When a guy sneaks away to steal a glimpse at the girls on the Web his heart starts to speed up. Adrenaline rushes through his body, and the physical enjoyment of what he is looking at causes him to forget almost everything around him, except, of course, the fact that someone might interrupt his virtual rendezvous. So he keeps his eyes glued to the screen and his ears alert for anyone who might catch him.

What are some ways that modern technology is increasing Satan's ability to tempt people sexually? How can you avoid such temptation?

The guys who "graduate" from the Web to an actual girlfriend feel the same rush times a zillion when they start crossing sexual boundaries. The problem, as you know, is that the feeling is brief, but the regret lasts a lifetime. The Bible describes it as the "passing pleasures of sin" in Hebrews 11:25. Think about it, it probably feels great to use crystal meth...for the few minutes you are using it. But then your hair begins to fall out, open sores that won't heal show up all over your body, your teeth literally fall out of your head, and your skin cracks and peels off in large chunks. And if you continue to use it, you die in about three years. Needless to say, the few minutes of enjoyment aren't worth the lasting consequences of a tortured, extremely brief life. In truth, sex is awesome in the marital relationship for which it was designed. But outside that relationship it is toxic. It is like radioactive material. You can use it constructively to power nuclear plants and produce billions of dollars worth of useful energy. But if you expose a person to it outside of its protective boundaries, it blasts him with harmful rays that rapidly destroy his body.

What does yielding to sexual temptation cost you—emotionally, physically, and spiritually?

The Only Relationship That Can Save You

The fact of the matter is, you know sexual temptation is coming. In our technological age of instant communication there is no possible way to avoid the Marianas who are out there. So what is the solution, how can you stay pure in such a sexually filthy world? First, you must understand the cost of sin. If you can picture Christ hanging on the cross, with nails driven through His hands and feet, a crown of thorns dripping blood down his face, and a back that was shredded by scourging, then you can see the cost of sin. More than what pornography or fornication can do to your body and spirit,

Read 1 Corinthians 6:18. What do you think is different about sexual sin from other sins?

you must think about how painful it is to God. It truly breaks His heart. I'm convinced that you will not be able to avoid sexual sin unless you can think like Joseph did. When Potiphar's wife tried to get him to have sex with her, he refused and said: "How then can I do this great wickedness, and sin against God?" (Genesis 39:9). The desire to please your heavenly Father and make Him proud of your pure life is the only real motivating factor that will keep you away from pornography and sex before marriage.

A Game Plan

Even with the desire to please your heavenly Father, you need a strategy, a game plan. After all, Joseph ran away from Potiphar's wife when he was tempted. You know that Satan is going to throw everything he has at you. So here are some practical suggestions that can help you defeat temptation.

- **Pray**–Because prayer sounds so "religious," we often fail to realize the practical value of talking to God when we are tempted. In the model prayer, Jesus showed us how to ask God to help us fight temptation (Matthew 6:13). When you find yourself in a tempting situation, ask God to help you out. He will.

- **Toss the Tempter**–If there is something in your life that keeps tripping you up, get rid of it. I know smart phones are super cool, and the apps are amazing. But if you find that you are looking at stuff you shouldn't on your phone, scale back to one that doesn't connect to the Internet. Also, if you have a computer in your room that is tempting you, toss it. I don't mean throw it away, just put it in an open place in your house where it is much more difficult to be alone with it. "Run away" from "alone time" with the Tempter just like Joseph did. In the movie *Fireproof*, the husband who was addicted to pornography took a baseball bat and smashed his computer into smithereens when he finally decided to repent. That may sound drastic, but it might be exactly what you need to do with whatever media is tripping you up.

> Read Proverbs 7:6-23. Identify the ways that the "crafty harlot" tempted the young man to sexual sin.

- **Practical Tips for Not Going too Far**–When it comes to a relationship with a girlfriend, there are some really simple rules that would help keep you sexually pure. Here are a few:

- Don't put your hands under any of her clothes. Simple enough. Just tell yourself that your hands will never go up anything or down anything that a girl is wearing until you are married.

- Don't touch anything that would be covered by a swimsuit, even outside of clothes. Don't get me wrong, I'm not saying that modern swimsuits are modest. All I'm saying is that if a swimsuit would cover it, then decide you won't touch it at all, until you are married.

- Kiss standing up. Lying down on anything like a couch or bed will certainly tempt you to do other things. Make a personal rule that you kiss standing up.

• Kiss quick. This one thing I know, prolonged sessions of kissing that can last for an hour are sure to be a stumbling block. The old "we're watching a movie on the couch by ourselves, but after it's over, we couldn't tell you a single scene of it," won't help you. There is no Biblical rule that states, "kiss only for 5 seconds at a time while dating." But if you will decide to limit your kissing to quick kissing before you are married, you'll be a lot happier. [NOTE: Some young men and women have decided that they are not going to kiss anyone on the lips until they get married. I'm not saying that the Bible commands that, and I certainly don't think that all lip-kissing before marriage is sinful. But I will tell you this, I've never seen a person who decided to wait be disappointed or sorry for the decision.]

Read Proverbs 6:27-28. What is the Proverbs writer trying to say about sexual sin in those verses?

Conclusion

God loves you and he wants sex to be awesome for you in marriage. Satan hates you and wants to ruin your life. He wants you to have a few minutes of fun, exciting, physical pleasure that will cost you pain, suffering, and (he hopes) your soul. Satan wants you to be emotionally tormented and messed up (1 Peter 5:8). Your only hope to defeat Satan is to realize that sin hurts your most important relationship—the one with your heavenly Father. Knowing that Satan has made it easy for you to get what will hurt you, you will have to decide on a personal strategy that will empower you to defeat his temptations. Each time you defeat his temptation, however, you will grow stronger. Satan's henchwomen, the Marianas of the world, will have less and less ability to pull you into their wickedness. Ultimately, your fight will pay-off when you receive the crown of life which the Lord has promised to all those who "endure" temptation (James 1:12).

What is the book of Song of Solomon about? What is God's view of sex?

KB

Tools for Real Men
Helping to measure up

~~ABS~~TINENCE OR SEX: CAN YOU AFFORD IT?

The material presented by Kyle Butt is designed for churches to use in combating the lies about sex that are perpetrated on our young people through the media, schools and friends. The seminar teaches God's plan of sexual abstinence before marriage. This material is very frank and explicit regarding the various kinds of sexual diseases that can result from participation in those activities.

abstinenceorsex.com

THE TRUTH ABOUT PORNOGRAPHY

Can Christians engage in viewing pornography? Sooner or later, most of us find ourselves facing moral, social, and ethical situations that command our attention. These situations can affect our family, friends, neighbors or others. In an easy-to-understand manner, Don Blackwell presents a compelling and informative answer from a biblical and practical standpoint.

video.wvbs.org

THE TRUTH ABOUT DANCING

Can Christians participate in modern dancing? What are the moral implications involved? In an easy-to-understand manner, Don Blackwell presents a compelling and informative answer from a biblical and practical standpoint.

video.wvbs.org

CHAPTER 11

The Second Biggest Decision of Your Life

"A REAL man, the kind of man a woman wants to give her life to, is one who will respect her dignity, who will honor her like the valuable treasure she is. A REAL man will not attempt to rip her precious pearl from its protective shell, or persuade her with charm to give away her treasure prematurely, but he will wait patiently until she willingly gives him the prize of her heart. A REAL man will cherish and care for that prize forever." (Leslie Ludy)

"Who can find a virtuous wife? For her worth is far above rubies. The heart of her husband safely trusts her; so he will have no lack of gain. She does him good and not evil all the days of her life." (Proverbs 31:10-12)

I had seen the ad in the paper for a truck that was for sale. I called the guy who owned it, Keith, as I recall. We arranged a time to meet so that I could check it out. We met, I looked the truck over, and asked if I could test drive it. He said that was fine and hopped in the passenger's seat. We were just going around the block, but it was enough time to get into a conversation about his family and church background. I asked him where he went to church, and he explained that he grew up in the church of Christ, but he had married a woman who was not a member of the Church, and he was now going with her to church. The church he attended with her was not a religious group that is faithful to the Lord. I was not surprised to hear that he had left the Lord's Church when I heard that he had married a woman who was a member of another religion. This story could be told a billion times over: A faithful follower of God marries a non-Christian and loses his soul to follow his wife. Such a sad, but, oh so common, occurrence.

As I hope you can tell by now, the second most important decision you will ever make is who you will marry. I say second, of course, because the most important decision you will ever make is becoming a

Read 1 Corinthians 15:33. What does this verse have to do with this chapter?

Christian. Who you will marry, however, is so vital that it often is the deciding factor in a person's eternal destiny. I was talking about this subject with a friend of mine in Montgomery, Alabama, and he went so far as to say that for some people, he thought who they married was the most important decision. He said this because he had seen so many people, especially men, go whichever way their wives went. While I would still rank it second, it is a close second.

In theory, it is not a decision that every person makes. Some people choose not to marry. They may choose to remain single because they like the single lifestyle better. They may choose single life because it gives them more freedom to work in the Lord's Kingdom. Or it could be that they never find the right spouse. Nobody says that you have to get married. In fact, the apostle Paul told the Corinthians that, due to the distress during their time, it was better for them if they remained unmarried (1 Corinthians 7:26). Our Lord Jesus Christ was not married, and neither was Paul. Marriage is not for everyone.

But realistically, most of you reading this book will get married. The last time I checked, 98% of all Americans get married. We are not under the same distressing conditions as the Corinthians, and marriage is the path most every one of you will choose. And it is a great choice. God designed marriage in the Garden of Eden with the first man and woman, and it has been the foundation of every productive society since the dawn of human history. Marriage is great......if.

The Big 'If'

Marriage is wonderful, amazing, marvelous, enrapturing, exciting, rewarding, blissful, joyous, fulfilling......if. That little, two-letter word "if" carries a lot of weight. I assume you know what is coming after that word if...you choose the right spouse. If you don't, marriage is miserable, terrible, horrible, crippling, emotionally debilitating, and often leads to spiritual death. Who you choose to marry makes all the difference.

A Bad Woman is Nothing but Bad for You

It doesn't matter how bad you think being lonely is, it is not as bad as being connected to a bad woman. The Proverbs writer said: "Better to dwell in the wilderness (or desert), than with a contentious and angry woman" (Proverbs 21:19). I don't know if you have ever been to the desert. It is hot, dry, and miserable. I wouldn't want to spend a few days there, much less live there.

Why do you think it is so difficult to remain a faithful Christian if you marry someone who is not striving to be a faithful Christian?

But it would be better to live where there is hardly any water, the sun fries your skin, and the wild animals threaten you, than to live with a contentious woman. Earlier in that chapter, the writer said it is better to live in a corner of a housetop than with a contentious woman (21:9).

In Proverbs 19:13, the inspired writer said "the contentions of a wife are a continual dripping." Now don't miss that word picture. Think of a faucet that has a slow leak that drips about every 5 seconds...drip...drip...drip...drip. A while back I was lying in bed and heard such a drip. It was coming from my bathtub faucet. I attempted to ignore it...drip...drip...and just go...drip...to sleep, but I found myself...drip...thinking about when that...drip...nerve wracking...drip...sound was going to stop. Needless to say, I was up late that...drip...night trying to fix the situation because...drip...there was no peace while the faucet dripped.

Samson got a taste of this continual dripping and it cost him his life. He fell in love with a bad woman who wanted to learn the secret of his great strength. She wanted to sell this secret to the Philistines for lots of money. She begged him for the secret. She pleaded. She cajoled. She connived. She dripped. So much so that the Bible says: "And it came to pass, when she pestered him daily with her words and pressed him, so that his soul was vexed (impatient to the point of) to death, that he told her all his heart" (Judges 16:16-17). Samson fell in love with a Philistine woman who cared more about money than she cared about Samson or his God. Her continual dripping cost him his life. You can easily imagine how a modern day "dripping" scenario would go between a Christian and his non-Christian wife.

Modern Day Contentious Wife: "I don't think it is fair that the children always have to go to your church. What is so special about your church? You are so arrogant. You think that your church is the only church that is teaching right. You are so judgmental, judging my church and all the other religions. You teach about love and God, but you can't love God if you judge people and tell them they are going to hell. What will our kids think if you tell them that I'm not saved? That can't be good for a family: for the kids to think their mom is going to hell. What kind of husband would pull his family apart like that? You can't love me and tell the kids that the people in my religion are going to hell. That isn't love. Why don't you just ease up a little and come with me every now and then? You don't have to join my church, just don't tell the kids it's wrong...."

> **What are some of the areas you can imagine being problems in your life if you marry someone who does not love the Lord?**

You can see what a man would be up against in such a situation. In the real world, most men cave in to the pressure and lose their soul in an effort to find a little "peace" in their homes. Unfortunately, they never find the peace they are looking for.

The Tragic Tale of the World's Wisest Man

God appeared to King Solomon and gave him a wish. Solomon could have anything in the world he wanted. At the time, Solomon's wish list was perfectly aligned with God's desires. Solomon wanted wisdom. He wanted the ability to know the difference between right and wrong. Because of Solomon's humble request for wisdom, God made him the wisest man in the world, as well as the richest. He had wealth beyond our imagination. During his reign, there was so much gold and silver in his palace, that silver was considered to be as common as rocks (1 Kings 10:27). You would think that Solomon would certainly be among those who remained faithful to God. But he wasn't. Even with all his wisdom, his heart was turned away from God.

How in the world, you may wonder, could the wisest man in the world turn away from God? He married the wrong women—as simple as that. God had warned the Israelites not to marry foreign women who worshipped idols. But Solomon didn't listen. In my opinion, one of the saddest passages of all Scripture is found in 1 Kings 11:4-6:

> *"For it was so, when Solomon was old, that his wives turned his heart after other gods; and his heart was not loyal to the Lord his God, as was the heart of his father David.*

What does the story of Solomon tell you about the power of a persuasive woman?

> *For Solomon went after Ashtoreth the goddess of the Sidonians, and after Milcom the abomination of the Ammonites. Solomon did evil in the sight of the Lord, and did not fully follow the Lord, as did his father David."*

Can you imagine the wisest man in the world, the man who wrote the Bible books of Ecclesiastes, Song of Solomon, and most of Proverbs, bowing down to a statue? It seems absurd. The living God had appeared to him twice, talked to him, and given him all his heart desired. Yet Solomon's wives turned him away from the Lord. It is ironic that Solomon wrote so much about the contentious wife, yet he allowed his heart to be turned by female persuasion.

So How Do You Pick Her?

I hope you can see that picking the wrong woman can be eternally costly. But we haven't looked at many positive ways to pick a wife. What characteristics do you need to be looking for in a wife? Here is a brief, but important list of things to consider:

1) She loves the Lord more than she loves you. If she seeks God first (Matthew 6:33), she will be a happy, fulfilled person who can spread love and joy to those around her. If she is not in love with God, she cannot know how to be in love with you.

Read Proverbs 31:10-31. What traits does the virtuous woman have that would make being her husband desirable?

2) She reads her Bible and prays. You might think this sounds cliché, but think about it. If she is constantly listening to God tell her to do to others

as she would want them to do to her, won't she treat her husband great? If she knows she would like love, affection, and consideration, she will be more apt to give these things to her husband, because she is listening to God. Trust me when I say a girl who is obedient to God becomes a wife who blesses her husband.

3) She cares more about her heart than her hair. Our culture is a visually-oriented, sexually-driven rat race that tells girls they are not pretty enough—regardless of how pretty they are. Since God sees the heart, He knows how useless it is to focus too much attention on looks. Throughout the Bible, the woman who is viewed as virtuous spends more of her resources focusing on her heart than her hair, wardrobe, or looks (read Proverbs 31:10-31 and 1 Peter 3:3-4).

4) She is content with what she has. Paul explained to Timothy that "godliness with contentment is great gain" (1 Timothy 6:6). He also explained that those who desire to be rich and are not content pierce "themselves through with many sorrows" (1 Timothy 6:10). A discontented woman is like rottenness in a man's bones (Proverbs 12:4).

5) She will let you be the head of your house. It is very unpopular today for husbands to be the head of their houses. In fact, our society teaches that, at the least, a house should be a democracy where everyone has an equal vote. That is not how God designed the home. He appointed men to love their wives as Christ loved the Church. And He appointed

> **What are some ways a woman who does not love God can bring harm or shame on her husband and family?**

them to be the heads of their homes (Ephesians 5:22). That means you need to find a girl who will let you be the head of the home. It does not mean you find a girl who will let you boss her around. That is not what it means to submit. It means you find a girl that respects the role of the husband as God designed it and who will encourage you to be the leader of your home (1 Peter 3:3-7). One good way to see if she respects the position of a husband is to watch how she treats her dad.

6) She is kind. Wit might be captivating. And beauty might be alluring. But kindness heals the soul, builds character, and fosters joy. "She opens her mouth with wisdom, and on her tongue is the law of kindness" (Proverbs 31:26).

I once heard a story about a Christian wife who tried to convert her husband. He hated the church and did everything he could to keep her from attending. In fact, he was verbally abusive and terribly mean. One Sunday morning his wife was dressed for church and on her way out the door. He stood in her way with a pistol pointed at her head and told her she was not going to church that Sunday. She looked him right in the eyes and said "Either you shoot me and I'm going to heaven, or I'm going to church." He later was converted to Christ. That is the kind of woman you need to marry.

Discuss the statement: You generally marry someone who is as moral as you are. What do you think you need to be in order to attract a girl who will make a godly, enjoyable, worthy wife?

KB

Tools for Real Men
Helping to measure up

CHRIST-CENTERED MARRIAGE

Your marriage is not just about your happiness, but your holiness. No matter how good or how bad your marriage relationship might be right now, if Christ is your focus your marriage will improve. Marriage is not so much about you and your spouse, but about you and your God. Join Mike Vestal as he presents practical steps from Colossians chapter 3 on how to have a Christ-centered marriage.

video.wvbs.org

CHRIST-CENTERED FAMILY

On loan – those two words vividly and powerfully describe your family and your home. Our families are ours for a while, so that they can be God's forever. How important it is to be trustworthy and loyal with God's greatest earthly gift: our family. Join Mike Vestal as he takes an in-depth look at how God's word teaches us to be stewards of our family.

video.wvbs.org

MAN'S ROLE IN MARRIAGE: A STUDY IN LEADERSHIP

This video is the second in a program of three lessons on building and maintaining marriages and families according to God's plan. In this lesson, Steve Springer presents "Man's Role in Marriage: A Study in Leadership." Through God's Word, we have the standard for defining the role of a husband and father. When this role is followed, families and relationships work harmoniously.

video.wvbs.org

76

CHAPTER 12

"Work" is NOT a Four Letter Word

"Make it a life-rule to give your best to whatever passes through your hands. Stamp it with your manhood. Let superiority be your trademark." (Orison Swett Marden)

"Whatever your hand finds to do, do it with all your might...." (Ecclesiastes 9:10)

Well, of course we know, technically speaking, the word "work" is spelled with four letters. But by the way some guys treat the word, you would think it was as profane as "real" four-letter words. In fact, in some ways, our society tries to make us think that work is something to be avoided like the plague. We hear about get-rich-quick schemes that require little effort and pay big dividends. Spam e-mails offer us a 100% guarantee that if we try their plan or product we can retire at age 32 and never have to work another day in our lives. As teens, you are informed that you have your whole life to work, now is the time to take it easy, relax, enjoy your teen years, and shun work like it's a rabid dog. Is work really that bad, something to be put off, to shy away from as long as possible? From the title of this chapter, you know that the answer to this question is a big fat "NO." Let's explore why work is something you can really get into.

Keeping the Wolves Away From the Door

No doubt you've heard the story since you were a kid of the three little pigs. The three pigs ramble off into the world to make

their fortunes. The first pig hates work so he builds his house of straw; second pig doesn't like work much either so he makes his out of sticks. The third pig likes to feel safe in his house, so he builds his house out of bricks. By and by the big bad wolf comes along and blows down the houses of the first and second little pigs and they race as fast as their porky little legs will carry them to their brother's brick house. The wolf can't blow that house down, tries to get in through the chimney, and gets a burned backside as a reminder of what chimneys are used for. Of course, the moral of the story is that work keeps wolves away from your door, and it helps you feel safe and secure.

Now, most of us have in our minds the idea that when God created Adam and Eve, He placed them in the beautiful Garden of Eden to live a life of ease and leisure—with no work to do at all. But that is not how it was. When God created Adam and Eve, He placed them in the Garden of Eden "to tend and to keep it" (Genesis 2:15). The word "tend" means to "cultivate." They were designed to enjoy seeing how their hands and ingenuity could make the world a wonderful place. When they sinned, God cursed Adam to a life of much harder labor, but work was always a part of God's plan. Work was not a curse, it was a part of the original creation that God said was "very good".

That is why, when you go to the book of Proverbs, the text says: "In all labor there is profit, but idle chatter leads only to poverty" (14:23). There was a time when I might have argued with the validity of this verse. Let me explain. When I was about 14, my dad had a "job" for me and my two brothers. He told us to go pick up rocks out of a field that was about 10 acres. When we saw the field, and the rocks, we were stunned. Have you ever seen how many rocks one 10-acre field can hold? Just when you think you have cleared a two-foot-wide section of field, you pick up a foot-ball sized rock to see that it gave birth to four baseball-sized rocks hiding underneath it. And underneath those rocks is a quaint little nest of eight more

Think of a time when you have done your best on a successful job. How did that make you feel?

golfball-sized rocks, etc. We worked for countless hours picking up bazillions of rocks. We knew we would never be able to pick up all those rocks. And, guess what, we never did. To this day there are still rocks in that field. In fact, I was taking my three-year-old son on a ride through the rock-strewn field the other day. I had him get off and pick up a rock (there are still plenty to choose from), just so I could say that the third generation of Butt boys has picked up rocks in that same field. Of course, when I was a teen I thought, "What a waste of time"...or was it? Every rock we picked up made us stronger, got our blood pumping, kept us off the couch, helped us be better football and basketball players, helped keep our minds off junk, and gave us a sense of accomplishment. In all labor there is profit.

Think of a time when you were lazy and only half-heartedly applied yourself. How did that make you feel?

The story is told of a farmer who was raising seven sons. He worked them hard on the farm, feeding cows, hauling hay, bringing in eggs, building fences, and a thousand other things that "needed" doing on the farm. One of his neighbors saw the way he was working his boys and accosted him: "Farmer, you don't need to work those boys that hard to raise crops and cows. You could do it with a lot less work." The farmer looked at him briefly and replied, "I'm not raising cows, I'm raising boys." In all labor there is profit.

Worse Than an Infidel

Some time ago a notorious atheist named Christopher Hitchens died of cancer at the age of 62. He was famous for a book titled 'gOD Is Not Great,' in which he blasphemed the God of the Bible in words that we would not use to describe the dirtiest dog. He was an infidel, an unbeliever, whose life was spent in complete rebellion against God and who is forever going to reap the reward of the wickedness that he sowed during his brief life. It would be worse than a tragedy for any one of you reading this book to live such a reckless, corrupt life. Yet, before we get carried away decrying the wasted life of an infidel, there is something you should know. There are some things that, in God's eyes, are worse than the rebellion of infidelity. In 1 Timothy 5:8 we read: "But if anyone does not provide for his own, and especially those of his household, he has denied the faith and is worse than an unbeliever."

Did you hear that? Can you believe it? If an able-bodied man is not willing to work to supply the needs of his own house, he is worse than an unbeliever. I would hate to stand at the Judgement Seat of God on the final day and be in Christopher Hitchens' shoes. But as odd as it may sound, I would be even more terrified to know that I refused to do the work that God had designed me to do. Why do you think that God said: "Blessed are the dead who die in the Lord from now on...that they may rest from their labors and their works follow them" (Revelation 14:13)? Those who enter heaven will have been working on Earth and will be looking for a place and time to rest. But that place and time is not while they are on Earth. [Don't misunderstand, we are not advocating workaholicism, we are simply saying that work is good, in all work there is profit, God designed us to work, and a man who refuses to do his share is worse in God's sight than an atheist.]

> **Why do you think that God views laziness and the refusal to work as being a worse sin than being an infidel?**

Brother to A Great Destroyer

Picture this, there is a evil villain who has his warped mind set on killing a great number of people. He devises a scheme whereby he loosens a bolt on a railroad car. That bolt is the one that holds the passenger cars to the engine. If it does not hold, the cars get disconnected and the passengers in the cars race at breakneck speed down the hill and plummet to their deaths. Sounds demented and dastardly, wouldn't you say? Now picture this, a guy working in

> **Why do you think that people who feel useless are often depressed?**

a factory doesn't take his job very seriously. He is just there for the buck he gets paid, and he doesn't think he owes his employer a thing. The fact that he is there should be enough, and he feels little, if any responsibility, for the finished product. He happens to be the one who is hired to put the bolt on the railroad car that holds the lead car to the engine. He is lazy and does his job haphazardly. He puts the bolt on wrong, the cars get disconnected and...you know the rest of the story. Listen to Proverbs 18:9: "He who is slothful in his work is a brother to him who is a great destroyer." The villain in our little story wanted to kill people. The factory worker was just lazy. But the result was the same, lots of people died. That is why the Proverbs writer could say that a lazy person is the brother of one who intends to destroy.

You've heard the old saying, if a job is worth doing, then it's worth doing right. In Ecclesiastes 9:10 we read: "And whatever your hand finds to do, do it with your might." If you work in a factory and put in bolts for a living, then you be the best bolt assembly technician you can be. When I was growing up, my mother always told me that I could be anything in the world I wanted to be. And if it turned out that I wanted to be a solid waste disposal engineer (we used to call them garbage men) that was great, as long as I was the best garbage man I could be.

Work is Work

In all work there is profit, and there are many different kinds of work. When we think about work, we often visualize factory work, or working on a farm, or cutting grass, retail sales, etc. There are varying jobs, and often the mental, spiritual work is just as difficult as manual labor such as hauling hay or working in a factory. In fact, there are lots of people who are willing to do manual labor but will not apply themselves to do difficult mental or spiritual work. There are many who would rather haul bricks for

What were some of the jobs great men of the Bible had? How did their jobs prepare them for what God had planned for them?

10 hours a day than study a book and get an education. When we look into the Bible we see many different jobs being commended by God. For instance, the apostle Paul said that it is right and good for preachers who "labor" in the Gospel to get paid for their job (1 Corinthians 9:9-14). [It is also interesting to note that while Paul commended paying preachers, he also worked with his hands to support himself by making tents.] People often joke that preachers work for three hours a week, two on Sunday and one on Wednesday night. But the Bible says that preparing lessons, teaching, and studying God's Word is hard work.

In Acts 6:1-7, the early Church had a problem. Some of the widows were being left out of the daily distribution of food for the needy. The apostles knew that somebody needed to see to this work and take care of the widows. But it might surprise you to know that the apostles said they were not going to do the job of caring for the widows, but instead were going to give themselves "continually to prayer and to the ministry of the word" (Acts 6:4). The apostles were hard at work preaching and praying, and it was just as valuable a work as distributing food to the poor. In Colossians 4:12, Paul's companion, Epaphras, sent his greetings to the Colossians. Paul noted that this faithful man was "always laboring fervently" for the Colossians "in prayers." Epaphras "labored fervently in prayer." God has created us each to do a job that we are specifically designed to do. Let's get to work.

A Job Well Done

One day, if you have been faithful in your work and service to the Lord, you will hear the most welcome words that any mortal could imagine: "Well done, good and faithful servant, enter into the joys of the Lord." The fact is, there is nothing like the feeling of being a faithful servant, of a job well done. We can tell you from experience that there is just something about looking at a barn filled with hundreds of square bales of

> What reason does Paul give in Ephesians 4:28 for why we ought to work?

hay neatly stacked to the ceiling, knowing that you had a hand in moving every one of them. There is nothing like flipping through the pages of a freshly printed book that you spent hundreds or thousands of hours researching, writing, proofreading, rewriting, reproofreading and getting to press.

Not many years ago there was a fine Christian young man who had fallen in love with a fine Christian young woman. Everything seemed perfect, and then tragedy struck. The young lady was diagnosed with a very serious form of cancer. Throughout the entire ordeal, the young man was by her side, never faltering, always there for her. One older Christian lady commended the young man for his faithfulness to her. His response was classic. He simply said, "I'm just doing my job." That is what a Christian man does—his job.

KB

Tools for Real Men
Helping to measure up

MY GOD AND HIS MONEY

This captivating 6-lesson DVD series is designed to help Christians understand their responsibility as stewards of the Lord's money. In the process, they will also learn that it truly is more blessed to give than to receive. Lessons Include: (1) Stewardship, (2) Purpose in Your Heart, (3) Benefits Of Giving Liberally, (4) Money: Powerful & Dangerous, (5) Proof of Your Love, and (6) Sowing & Reaping.

www.wvbs.org

THE TRUTH ABOUT...GIVING

How can the church, as a whole, benefit from the offerings freely given by Christians? We live in a world of religious confusion. Worship has become more about the individual than about God. But in the midst of the confusion, the Bible remains clear. Don Blackwell and Neal Pollard deal with basic principles of worship in a simple and concise manner that rings true to the Word of God. Whether a new convert or a diligent seeker of truth, these lessons will benefit and strengthen you.

video.wvbs.org

THE TRUTH ABOUT BIBLE STUDY

How can Christians provide reasoned answers and guidance to friends without proper study and contemplation? We live in a world of religious confusion. Worship has become more about the individual than about God. But in the midst of the confusion, the Bible remains clear. Don Blackwell and Neal Pollard deal with basic principles of worship in a simple and concise manner that rings true to the Word of God.

video.wvbs.org

HOW TO READ THE BIBLE

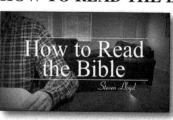

The Bible is a complex library of 66 books, and for the newcomer it may seem overwhelming. These 66 books tell a story. This study is a simple introduction to the different kinds of literature, and provides strategies for reading. The aim is to encourage the reader to read their Bible without being overwhelmed. Join Steven Lloyd in this great study, which is meant for any Bible reader.

video.wvbs.org

CHAPTER 13

WANTED:
Real Men

"Let men see, let them know, a real man, who lives as he was meant to live." (Marcus Aurelius)

"Be watchful, stand firm in the faith, act like men, be strong." (1 Corinthians 16:13)

Blazing guns, damsels in distress, and fast horses…it just doesn't get much better than a good ol' western when it comes to movies, especially when the whole plot of the story is revenge. I know, "'Vengeance is mine, I will repay,' says the Lord." But, there's just something about all that gun-fighting, fist-fighting, horse-riding action that makes a man wish he could've lived in a different time. I'm talking about a time when a man worked long, hard hours on the ranch to provide for his family. He would come home and his wife would greet him with love and pride in the man that he was. I'm talking about a time when dads taught their boys about life by taking them into the wild and teaching them to hunt and work cattle. I'm talking about a time when integrity was a way of life. You see all of this portrayed in great western movies. But let's face it…a western is not a western unless a gang of bad-guys rides into town and starts bullying the land-owners and farmers. Enter the cool stuff—gunfights, damsels in distress, and fast horses. Somebody has to save the town from the bad guys. Somebody has to get revenge. But who?

Have you ever noticed that there seems to be a shortage of good guys in these movies? All kinds of bad guys; not many good guys. The faces of these hoodlums with the word "WANTED" written at the bottom of the page are posted all over town, but no one seems to know what a good guy ought to look like. As a matter of fact, it seems like it would be more beneficial to everyone if the "WANTED" poster were for the one good guy that was needed instead of for all the bad guys...everyone knows the bad guys. Anyway, in rides John Wayne or Clint Eastwood, the hard-core cowboy, to save the day. This guy is the real deal, and you know it by his swagger. He can shoot; he can fight; he can ride. His job is to save the day, the damsel, and the entire town from the bandits—outnumbered 10 to 1. By the end of the movie, you're thinking, "that dude is THE MAN!"

What is your favorite "REAL MAN" movie? Why?

Our society has painted many different pictures of what THE MAN is. We've always heard things like, "Real men don't cry," or "Real men wear pink." We see commercials that portray the real man as the one with the beer and the babe, or wearing a certain cologne that makes him instantaneously irresistible. We see men on magazines with bulging muscles or million dollar suits. The difficulty with all of these ideals is that no individual man can live up to every single one of these prerequisites in order to become a "real man." And yet, each of these ideals is supposed to give us power. So which one do you choose to pursue? How can you say that one is more important that the rest? Which of these ideals becomes attainable?

What are some other ideas in our culture of what a "REAL MAN" ought to be or look like?

The truth is that if a man measures his manhood by some socially defined ideal, he will always find himself lacking. There will always be someone who is quicker on the draw. Girls DO NOT flock to boys because of beer or cologne. There will always be someone with bigger muscles or a fancier suit. Oh, and girls wear pink, too.

So, let's talk straight for a moment. If society's pictures of manhood are, by and large, unattainable or irrational, then there must be a more worthwhile, attainable reality of manhood that one can pursue.

In His Image

Enter God's purpose for man. While God gave us good looks, manly smells, and rock-hard emotions, He never intended for us to get hung up on these things. Even though He encased us in flesh and bone, His greatest desire is that we would understand our likeness in His image and seek Him. He longs for us to internalize the life of the real man named Jesus in both relationship and behavior. He wants us to live in such a way that when people look at us, they see Jesus and our love for Him.

Let me attempt to describe this idea of image in another way. When you think "Gatorade," who or what do you think about? What about Nike? When you hear the name Peyton Manning, what comes to mind? How about Tiger Woods? Companies work awfully hard to come up with specific logos that will represent their product in a way that invades your mind. They even pick big name athletes or actors to represent their products because of mankind's admiration for the elite. Because of this, they hope, and even expect, that their spokesperson will be very careful how he portrays himself in all areas of life. The company knows that their product is tied to the person's recognition and reputation. Image sells. On the flipside, when a person taints his reputation, everyone immediately has a hard time saying anything nice about him. Product sales suffer. He may have a great game in the arena, but he messed up big. He ruined his image.

You want to look like a real man? Make sure that you are tied up in God's image and that His image is tied up in you. When people think about God, they ought to think of your face, the face of a godly man. When people see your face, they ought to be encouraged to contemplate an amazing God. You see, God is what being real is all about in this life. If we make the constant decision to live in His image, then people will see what being a real man is all about, and they will see God. I wonder if people's perceptions of God are all too often inaccurate, because they don't see enough real men portraying His real image.

Can you think of some other notable figures that have ruined their reputation? How do you feel about them now?

Maybe that's why you've read every page of this book so far. Maybe you see the need for God's people to be more. Maybe you are looking to better equip yourself with knowledge and spirit in such a way that your manhood speaks volumes about your relationship with

God. I truly hope so, and I pray that everything in this book has been beneficial to your growth as a man of God. You see, in every aspect of life—purity, speech, actions, relationships, etc.—God wants you to be a real man.

Do you think it's easier to attain society's definition of a "REAL MAN" or God's? Why?

What's so cool about all of this—even if it seems overwhelming—is that God's image in your life is very attainable and rational. He has already equipped us with everything we need for this manhood: His image, His reconciliation, His power. All we need to do is embrace it!

By His Example

Jesus as a man, in the image of God, gives us the true picture of what a real man ought to look like. I do want to warn you, though, if you begin to look into the aspects of Jesus' life and if you try to portray them in yours, these things will not necessarily match up with society's misconceptions of a real man. However, if you are willing to internalize and incorporate the characteristics of Jesus into your life, you will undoubtedly find power, blessing, and fulfillment.

Jesus was all about power. He calmed a raging storm. He cured all kinds of diseases, often with just a touch of His hands. His words broke the power of the strongest demons. He walked on water. He made Lazarus come out of the grave after four days. He had the power of God, and He had no problem displaying it for all to see. But in His power, He displayed His love for mankind, His authority through meekness, and His ability to serve. Through these aspects of His life, He became the most amazing man this world has ever known.

Jesus' love for man is incomprehensible. Early in Jesus' ministry, He was in the temple reading from the prophet Isaiah, "The Spirit of the Lord is upon Me, because He has anointed Me to preach the gospel to the poor; He has sent Me to heal the brokenhearted, to proclaim liberty to the captives and recovery of sight to the blind, to set at liberty those who are oppressed; To proclaim the acceptable year of the Lord" (Luke 4:18-19). In a simple Old Testament passage, Jesus summarized

His entire mission to save mankind. Since before the foundations of the world, His most powerful motivation has been and always will be love—*agape* love. It is the reason for creation, and it is the reason for God's endless grace. Jesus loves us, because He is love. It doesn't matter what someone looks like or where he comes from. It doesn't matter what shortcomings an individual might have. Jesus' love for mankind is unconditional.

If we are ever going to be real men, we must learn this kind of love as well. We must make Jesus' mission of love our mission of love. This means that we take off our spiritual blinders of indifference and judgment. We get rid of our "cool factor," and we begin to treat people with the love Jesus has shown us. How will this look in your life? That's for you to decide in your individual relationships with the people in your life. I do know that it will have to include "joy, peace, patience, kindness, goodness, faithfulness, gentleness, and self-control." You just have to make sure you show everyone unconditional love.

Why do you think it is so difficult to show unconditional love on a daily basis?

Jesus' meekness is astonishing. Since we've just mentioned Jesus' power in the creation of the world...can you imagine the self-control needed to set aside that power and authority to such a degree that you make your way to the cross? Of course you can't...I can't either! But that's the meekness Jesus displayed in His example for us. Meekness is the decision to set aside power and strength in submission to God, and in most cases, it is shown in our relationships with others. Jesus once said, "Blessed (happy/fortunate) are the meek, for they shall inherit the earth." There were so many times in Jesus' ministry when He could have lashed out at His disciples. They were slow learners. And even though they lived with Him, they didn't always understand His purpose. How do you react when people don't understand you? If you're like me, you lash out in frustration, and all those around get to experience the power of your anger. Jesus was patient and gentle with people in these situations. Are you gentle in your treatment of those less fortunate or weak, or do you smirk out of disdain for their lowly circumstances and look down on them from your pedestal of possessions and abilities? Jesus touched these people and spent time with them. By the way, do your outward displays of power ever win people over? Do you ever build new relationships when you make the decision to remain elevated over others in your mind?

Paul wrote in Philippians 2 about the meekness and humility of Jesus that brought Him from His glory in Heaven to the humble state of a servant on this Earth. While the rest of our world believes that power is made in money, strength, and status, Jesus knew that the greatest power was to set self aside in an attempt to lift up all others. Oh, and I almost forgot about the meek inheriting the Earth. Philippians 2:9-11 says, "Therefore God also has highly exalted Him and given Him the name which is above every name, that at the name of Jesus every knee should bow, of those in heaven, and of those on earth, and of those under the earth, and that every tongue should confess that Jesus Christ is Lord, to the glory of God the Father." In the end, Jesus will be the Lord of every man, woman, and child who has ever been born. They will know and acknowledge His ultimate power and authority, because He displayed it in meekness and humility. You can begin to win hearts for God now, as you choose meekness in your treatment of others. That's power!

Jesus' service is unparalleled. It is meekness and humility that led Jesus to act in so many unfathomable ways. God, the Creator of all things, Who has the "whole world in His hands," did the job of a servant in John 13 and washed His disciples' feet. I'm not a feet person, so I have to react with "GROSS!" He did it anyway. On two separate occasions, He fed a grand total of 9,000 men (not counting women and children) with 12 loaves of bread and at least four fish. He treated an adulterous woman with dignity. He gave living water to a Samaritan woman. He spent an entire night in tears, sweat, and blood praying. He carried His own cross to the shameful hill. He rose again! Why? Service IS His mindset (Philippians 2:1-4). He always wants what is best for man, and in His power, He has done, and continues to do, everything possible to give us the best. When a man kneels in service, he is most powerful.

Is meekness the same thing as weakness? How does meekness show true character in a man's life?

In the end, people don't really care who has the biggest muscles or best suits. No one remembers what cologne you wore yesterday. At some point, the record books and trophy cases will be thrown away, and the man with the most money still dies. While John Wayne and Clint Eastwood are hard-core cowboys, Jesus "is the same yesterday, today, and forever," and He is the perfect image of God and man. He is powerful. He is real.

> What do you think true service looks like on a daily basis?

In His Kingdom

So what do you think? Are you ready to embrace the life of a real man? Are you ready to embrace His image in you and show others a different picture of a real man? Can you even begin to imagine what you could do in His kingdom with His power—the lives you could help change, the hearts you could help reach? Probably not! But with God it can happen!

> As you have read this book, what is the first thing you will begin to work on in your transformation into a "REAL MAN"?

God once used the word "good" to describe His satisfaction in creating man in His image. Let's strive for that description once more. I assure you that becoming a real man of God will be a different and awesome adventure. It will be challenging. But, you will succeed, because of the power of Jesus Christ being made known in your life. Above all, you will begin to fulfill God's purpose for your life on a daily basis as you grow from a boy to a man.

JDS

Additional Tools for Real Men

Would you like the ebook version?

An ebook version is available for most devices from World Video Bible School or the Amazon Kindle store (online or through your device).

WVBS.org
Amazon.com

Grow Your Bible Knowledge- For FREE!
School.WVBS.org

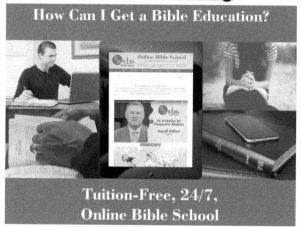

Other Great Resources

Apologetics Press
www.ApologeticsPress.org

House to House
www.HouseToHouse.com

Christian Courier
www.ChristianCourier.com

Gospel Broadcasting Network:
www.GBNTV.org

CPSIA information can be obtained
at www.ICGtesting.com
Printed in the USA
FFHW020209090119
50103136-54954FF